ANCESTRAL JEWELS

ANCESTRAL JEWELS

Diana Scarisbrick

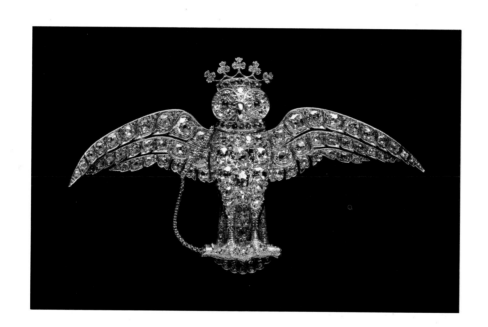

THE VENDOME PRESS

NEW YORK   PARIS

Published in the USA and Canada in 1990 by
The Vendome Press, 515 Madison Avenue, New York, NY 10022

Distributed in the USA and Canada by
Rizzoli International Publications
300 Park Avenue South, New York, NY 10010

First published 1989 by
André Deutsch Limited
105-106 Great Russell Street
London WC1B 3LJ

Library of Congress Cataloging-in-Publication Data
Scarisbrick, Diana.
    Ancestral jewels/by Diana Scarisbrick.
        p. cm.
    "First published 1989 by André Deutsch Limited . . . London"—T.p.
verso.
    Includes bibliographical references.
    ISBN 0-86565-119-1
    1. Jewelry—Great Britain—History. 2. Great Britain—Nobility.
I. Title.
    NK 7343.S3 1990   89-37354
    739.27'0941—dc20   CIP

Printed and bound in Spain by
Mateu Cromo Artes Graficas SA

Facing title page. Nineteenth-century jewels from the casket
of a noblewoman.

Title page. The Willoughby owl, paved with diamonds, with
ruby and sapphire collar and ducal coronet.

CONTENTS

ACKNOWLEDGEMENTS

I gratefully acknowledge permission to publish jewels and portraits in the possession of the following owners: their Graces the Dukes of Atholl, Buccleuch and Queensberry, Devonshire, Hamilton, Norfolk, Portland; the late Dukes of Northumberland and of St Albans; the Marquesses of Aberdeen, Bute, Londonderry, Tavistock; Grace, Countess of Dudley; Countess Mountbatten of Burma; the Earl and Countess of Rosebery; the Countess of Sutherland; the Earl of Yarborough; the late Lord Clifford of Chudleigh; Lord Mowbray, Segrave and Stourton; Baroness Willoughby De Eresby; the Viscount Hampden; Lady Mairi Bury; Lady Victoria Leatham; the Hon. Mrs Crispin Gascoigne; the Hon Robert Stonor; the Hon. Peter Ward; Mr John Berkeley; Mr Charles Cottrell-Dormer; Mr Michael Estorick; Major Malcolm Munthe M.C.; Mr Nigel Nicolson; Mrs A. Hornyold Strickland; Lady Abdy; the Administrative Trustees of the Chequers Estate; the National Trust; and those who prefer to remain anonymous.

Much useful information has been given by: Margaret, Duchess of Argyll, Miss Nancy Briggs FSA; Mr Simon Bull; Dr David Caldwell; Miss Debbie Colville; Mr John Cornforth; Mr Peter Day; Mr Michael Dillon; Captain Philip Grimes; the Hon. Harry Fane; Mr Christopher Gatiss; Dr Harford Montgomery Hyde; Mr John Jesse; Mr Alastair Lang; Mr Ian Lowe; Miss Lorna MacEchern; Mr Edgar Munhall; Mr Brian Nodes; Mr Eric Nussbaum; Mr Robin Muir; Mr Terence Pepper; Miss Rina Prentice; Miss Rosemary Rendel; Dr J.M. Robinson; Miss Barbara Scott; the Hon. Georgina Stonor; Mr Hugo Vickers; Mr Jonathan Volk; and Mr Gerard Watt.

I am also grateful to the photographers who have taken so much trouble on my behalf: Trevor Cris, Prudence Cuming, Desmond O'Neill, Christopher Phillips, John Reynolds, Ken Smith, Barry Swaebe, Robert Thrift and Robert Wilkins FSA.

Particular thanks are due to those friends who have been generous with their time and expertise: Mr Gerald Burdon for his comments on the text; Miss Mary Feilden of Christie's; Mr Martin and Mr Nicholas Norton of S.J. Phillips; Mr Peter Townend, social editor of the *Tatler*; and finally, my editor, Emma Manderson, for our happy collaboration.

PICTURE CREDITS

INTRODUCTION

Berkeley Castle in Gloucestershire (Plate 1), over-looking the waters of the Severn, is one of the few great English houses largely unaltered since the Middle Ages. Its grand, forbidding appearance gives no clue to the beauty of the family possessions within: these include the remarkable Hunsdon heirlooms, from Queen Elizabeth I's own jewel casket.

Berkeley Castle is not the only stately home where such jewels have survived, although their owners have been reluctant to publicise them for security reasons. Although their paintings, other works of art and furniture have been studied and recorded, the jewels which are equally part of the aristocratic heritage have been neglected until relatively recently.

In 1984 certain jewels were included in the Treasures of British Houses exhibition held in Washington DC. Caroline Knox of André Deutsch noticed the interest they generated, asked me to develop the theme into a book, and thereby sent me on a voyage of discovery which I would not have missed for the world. Hidden in strong rooms and in bank vaults I came across trophies of success – the jewelled badges of hereditary office, precious souvenirs of royal favour and of great historical events – and gems which were the insignia of wealth and social standing. Tucked away in jewel boxes I found heirlooms which, although intrinsically less valuable, were often exquisite, and always touching, mementoes of love, friendship and family affection. Most moving were the many memorials to martyrs for religious faith, to lives risked for the Stuart cause, or lost in duels and in battle.

It was also fascinating to trace the transformation of ancestral stones and pearls in accordance with fashion: although the settings change – often with each generation – the gems remain as emblems of family pride, visible links in the chain of history. Associated as they are with wealth and glory, with happiness and sorrow, these heirlooms bind us more closely to the past than any other of the relics which have come down to us. Like none other, they encompass the heights of human artistry and the breadth of human feeling. I hope that reading about them will bring you as much pleasure as their discovery has given me.

Diana Scarisbrick.

Plate 1. Berkeley Castle, Gloucestershire; home of the Hunsdon heirlooms, given by Queen Elizabeth to her cousin Henry.

One
THE TUDORS

Ancestral jewels are as much part of the British heritage as the stately home, the Gainsborough portrait and the thoroughbred racehorse. They enshrine family sentiment, and the desire to preserve them as heirlooms is at least as old as the Middle Ages. In 1432 Richard Earl of Arundel bequeathed his descendants the family jewels inherited from his father: 'a large pair of paternosters of gold [a rosary] with a gold brooch with certain other jewels and relics contained in a small strong box of white bound with silver with lions gilded...devised to me and to my heirs'. Continuing the custom, in 1530 the Tudor landowner John Sayer of Walsall left his gold chain, cross, brooch and signet as 'Arelomes perteyning ye sone and heir'. It is due to the tenacity of such men and women that we can still admire the family jewels that bind us so closely to the past.

Royal Gifts

Of all ancestral jewels, those of royal provenance were the most prized. In 1513 the rich mayor of London, Sir William Capel, ancestor of the Earls of Essex, asked his wife to entrust his gold chain – once owned by the young King Edward V, murdered in the Tower in 1483 – to their son Giles. For centuries a turquoise ring 'which King Henry VIII used to wear and was pictured with it on his forefinger' was preserved as one of the treasures of Holkham

Hall in Norfolk, itself one great work of art. Gifts from foreign monarchs were equally appreciated. Sir John Scott of Scott's Hall at Orlestone, who represented King Edward IV at the marriage of Princess Margaret of York with the Duke of Burgundy at Bruges in 1468, was given a diamond and ruby jewel which was passed down to his grandson who then left it to his daughter-in-law Elizabeth in 1594. In 1583 Thomas Earl of Sussex bequeathed his brother Henry the five gemstones from his rapier – a gift from the Emperor Maximilian whom he had invested with the Garter in 1567-8 – 'to remaine as a heirloome to the house for ever'.

These mementos were not always kept in cabinets as precious objects but might be worn by several generations in succession, as if by so doing the family might continue to enjoy the prestige of royal favour. Thus in 1674 the Countess of Pembroke bequeathed her daughter, the Dowager Countess of Thanet, her 'bracelet of little pomander beads set in gold and enamelling containing fifty seven beads in number which I usually weare under my stomacher: which bracelet is above 100 years old and was given by Philip II of Spain to Mary Queen of England and by her to my grandmother, Ann Countess of Bedford.'

Of the Tudor royal jewels which have survived the Hunsdon heirlooms are the most remarkable: a bracelet, a cameo, a girdle prayer book and a ship pendant which are still at Berkeley Castle in

Plate 2. Elizabeth Brydges, maid of honour to Queen Elizabeth
I, wearing a full parure of Renaissance jewellery in a portrait
painted by Hieronimo Custodis in 1589.

12

ÆTATIS SVÆ, 14 ....
ANNO DÑI, 1589 .....

Elizabeth Bruges daughter
to the Lord Giles Chandos

Hieronimo Custodis Antverpiensis
Fecit 8° July 1589

Gloucestershire. Queen Elizabeth gave them to her cousin Henry, first Lord Hunsdon, whose son George bequeathed them in 1603 to his daughter Elizabeth, wife of Sir Thomas Berkeley, to be preserved 'Soe long as the conscience of my heires shall have grace and honestie to perform my will for that I esteeme them right jeweles and monumentes worthie to be kept for their beautie, rareness and that for monie they are not to be matched nor the like yet known to be founde in this realme'.

The superb quality of the jewels fully vindicates Lord Hunsdon's pride in them. The unique rock crystal bracelet comes from the court workshops of the Emperor Akbar (d. 1603) in Agra or Delhi: it is the earliest surviving piece of Mughal jewellery in the world. The Emperor may have sent it to Queen Elizabeth as a gift and it is listed in her inventory of 1587: 'of rock crystal sett with sparckes of Rubies powdered and little sparckes of saphiers made hoopewise called Persia worke' (Plate 3). According to family tradition the ship pendant with green and white sails, armed with five cannons, represents the *Golden Hind* in which Sir Francis Drake sailed around the world in 1577-9. On deck Cupid places a wreath on the head of a man blowing a trumpet (Plate 4).

The miniature prayer book which Queen Elizabeth wore on a long chain hanging from her girdle, always close to hand, is an essentially English jewel, for John Lyly declared in *Euphues* (1578) that it was thanks to these jewelled prayer books that English women were 'as cunning in ye Scriptures' as Italian ladies − who preferred to carry fans − were well read in Ariosto and Petrarch. The front cover of the Hunsdon prayer book is set with a shell cameo of a young warrior, seen in profile amidst arabesques and rosettes (Plate 5). Inside is a manuscript recording the last prayer of the boy King Edward VI and the circumstances of his death:

The Prayer of Kynge Edward the VI which he made the VI of Julii 1553 and the VII yere of his raigne III houre before his dethe to him selfe his eyes being closed and thinkyne none had herd him the XVI yere of his age: 'Lord God deliver me out of this miserable wretched life and take me among they chosen. How be it not my will but they will be done. Lord I committ my spirit to the. O Lorde thou knowest how happie it were for me to be with

Plate 3 (*top*). Queen Elizabeth's rock crystal bracelet studded with cabochon rubies and sapphires: it is the earliest surviving piece of Mughal court jewellery.

Plate 4 (*above*). Enamelled gold pendent ship perhaps representing Sir Francis Drake's *Golden Hind*.

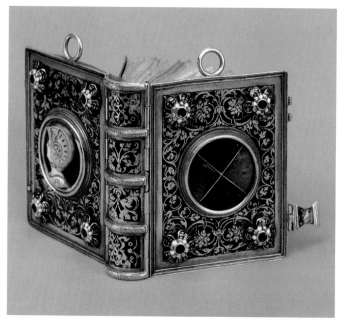

Plate 5 (*above*). Girdle prayer book containing the last prayer of King Edward VI, worn by Queen Elizabeth.

Plate 6 (*right*). Italian sardonyx cameo of Perseus rescuing Andromeda, set as a pendant.

thee. Yet for thy chosen sake send me life and helth that I may trulie serve the. O my Lord God save they chosen people of England. O my Lord God defend this realme from Papistrie and maintaine they trew religion that I and my peple may praise thy holy name'. Then turned he his face and seeing who was by him said unto them 'Are ye so nigh I thought ye had been farther ofe.' Then Dr. Owen said 'We heard you speke to your selfe but what ye saide we know not. He then after his fashion smiling he said I was praying to God. The last wordes of his prayers were thies 'I am fainte Lorde have mercy upon me and take my spirit'. And so he yelded up his gooste.

Only two other Tudor girdle prayer books have survived. One of them — also with black arabesques — was designed by Hans Holbein for Jane Hawte when she married the poet and courtier Sir Thomas Wyatt in 1537: it was left by the last male descendant of the Wyatts to his cousin Richard, second Earl of Romney. Exhibited at the Society of Antiquaries in 1723 as a great curiosity, it was published in *Archaeologia* (1873) by the Hon. Robert Marsham. The

other — now in the British Museum — was an heirloom of the Ashby family of Quenby in Leicestershire, given by George Ashby MP to his daughter-in-law Elizabeth in 1720. The biblical reliefs of the Judgement of Solomon and the Worship of the Golden Calf on the covers are attributed to the London workshop of the Flemish goldsmith, Hans of Antwerp, which flourished under royal patronage from 1540 to 1545.

The celebrated Hunsdon onyx cameo, set in an enamelled gold pendant worn from a chain, represents the mythological hero Perseus rescuing Andromeda. It illustrates marvellously the virtuoso talents of one of the best — albeit anonymous — hardstone engravers of the Renaissance. From the complex panorama of town and sea with ships and sea creatures, men and women stare in amazement as the young warrior flies down from the sky holding up the Gorgon's head on his shield and brandishing his sword. This tour-de-force matches the best engraving of the great cameo-cutters of ancient Greece and Rome (Plate 6).

Cameos and Miniatures

The Tudor monarchs revived the cameo for their official images. The important portraits of Henry VIII and his children – Edward VI, Mary I and Elizabeth I – in the Devonshire collection at Chatsworth are the sixteenth-century counterparts of those commissioned by the royal families of imperial Rome. But it is a later portrait, of Elizabeth as Queen, which has perhaps the most intriguing history. According to the Blencowe family tradition their ancestor, the extreme Protestant William Barbour, condemned to die at the stake by Queen Mary I, was reprieved by Queen Elizabeth whose first act on becoming queen had been to order the extinction of the fires burning at Smithfield for the execution of heretics. To celebrate his providential release Mr Barbour had a jewel made which he bequeathed to his eldest son with the request that the eldest daughter in each generation should be given the name of Elizabeth. He commissioned a pendant set with the Queen's cameo portrait framed in diamonds and rubies with pearls clustered like a bunch of grapes hanging below. The tree enamelled on the back recalls how Queen Elizabeth heard of her accession while seated under an oak in the garden at Hatfield House. Mrs Blencowe gave the Barbour pendant to the Victoria and Albert Museum in 1894, where it is exhibited beside a similar jewel Queen Elizabeth gave her goddaughter, Elizabeth Wild: this is on loan from her descendants. The eastern origin of the bright blue turquoise Wild cameo is emphasised by the Turkish ewer intaglio at the back of the Queen's portrait.

A smaller cameo portrait, set in a ring, evokes the tragic fate of the last and most romantic of Queen Elizabeth's favourites, Robert second Earl of Essex. She gave it to him on the eve of his brilliant expedition to Cadiz in 1596 as a token of her warmest regard. When Lord Essex fell from favour he foolishly incited a rebellion which was a fiasco and was condemned to death in 1601. In the hope that the Queen would relent he returned the ring as a plea for mercy, but the Countess of Nottingham made sure it never reached her. Through Lord Essex's daughter Lady Frances Devereux the ring descended down the Thynne family, who sold it in 1911: it has been in Westminster Abbey since 1927.

Nicholas Hilliard, who brought the English art of the portrait miniature to perfection, brilliantly fulfilled his responsibilities as official custodian of the Queen's image. His miniature of her is set in the locket she gave Sir Thomas Heneage of Copt Hall, Essex, which is not only exquisite in itself but politically significant. Sir Thomas was Treasurer of the armies levied to resist the Spanish Armada and the locket commemorates its defeat under the Queen's inspired leader-

Plate 7. The Gresley Jewel, a locket with cover set with a sardonyx cameo of a negress with white veil and lace collar.

16

ship. On the front her gold profile stands out like a medallion of a Roman empress: framed in rubies and diamonds, it is inscribed ELIZABETHA D.G. ANG. RRA. ET HIB. REGINA (Elizabeth by the Grace of God Queen of England France and Ireland). The ark floating on stormy seas enamelled on the back with the motto SAEVAS TRANQUILLA PER UNDAS (Peacefully through the stormy waves) alludes to her wise direction of the Ark of the English Church, as Defensor Fidei. The inscription encircling the dynastic Tudor rose enamelled on the inside of the lid HEI MIHI QUOD TANTO VIRTUS PERFUSA DECORE NON HABET ETERNOS INVIOLATA DIES (Alas that so much virtue diffused with beauty should not last inviolate for ever) by Walter Haddon, the Queen's Master of Requests, regrets that, like the rose, the Queen too must eventually pass away. Sir Thomas's descendants kept this locket for over three hundred years until it was sold at Christie's on 18 July 1902 to the millionaire American collector Pierpont Morgan. When it came up for sale again, this time at Sotheby's on 24 June 1935, the Heneage locket was presented by Lord Wakefield to the Victoria and Albert Museum.

Two more Hilliard miniatures of Queen Elizabeth were set in jewels which she gave Sir Francis Drake, and both have been preserved by his family. One is an opal and ruby sunburst jewel for his hat, set with a ruby intaglio globe commemorating his historic circumnavigation of the world in 1579. The other — which also contains the Queen's personal emblem of the phoenix — is a locket set with a sardonyx cameo of an African in profile beside a white woman, who wears a tiara to indicate her noble rank. The two busts personify Europe and Africa, or a legendary couple such as Othello and Desdemona. Sir Francis wears this jewel hanging from a gold chain in a portrait by Marcus Gheeraerts painted in 1595.

A similar locket is in the Pennington-Mellor-Munthe collection at Southside House, Wimbledon Common. Here the sardonyx cameo of a negress with white veil and collar set on the cover is framed in a garland of flowers interspersed with rubies and emeralds: it is flanked by two young black Cupids emerging from cornucopiae and shooting Love's arrows upwards (Plate 7). Inside there are miniatures by Nicholas Hilliard of Catherine Walsingham — cousin of Queen Elizabeth's Treasurer — and Sir Thomas Gresley of Drakelow in Derbyshire: the locket is thought to commemorate their marriage (Plate 8). It remained in the family until John Gresley lost it gambling at White's early this century, at which time it was acquired for the Southside collection.

Plate 8. The inside of the Gresley jewel: miniatures of Sir Thomas Gresley of Drakelowe, Derbyshire and his wife Catherine, by Nicholas Hilliard.

Baroque Pearls

The magnificent response of the Renaissance gold-smith to the challenge presented by the bizarre shapes of baroque pearls is demonstrated by two pendants at Chatsworth in Derbyshire. Both express grand concepts: in one a lion, king of the beasts, treads a snake underfoot (Plate 9), and the second is the noble head of a warrior crowned by a plumed helmet (Plates 10 and 11). The strangely shaped glistening silvery white pearls are perfectly integrated into the golden lion's muscular body and the curved outline of the helmet.

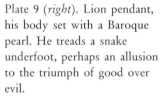

Plate 9 (*right*). Lion pendant, his body set with a Baroque pearl. He treads a snake underfoot, perhaps an allusion to the triumph of good over evil.

Plate 10 (*below left*). Pendent head of a warrior wearing a helmet set with a Baroque pearl.

Plate 11 (*below*). The back view of the warrior pendant, showing the diamond brooch pinned to the panache of plumes.

Narrative Jewels

The Renaissance jewellery which is now in the Exeter collection at Burghley House would also be at Chatsworth were it not for the unusually enlightened William third Earl of Devonshire, who died in 1684 leaving his widow Elizabeth 'All jewels, plates cabinett pictures and other things which she had bought for the furniture of her chamber and closett'. His will anticipated the Married Women's Property Act by two centuries, for Countess Elizabeth had absolutely no legal right to her own possessions without her husband's express permission. When she died they were removed to the apartments of her daughter Anne Countess of Exeter, at Burghley House: 'For (her) peculiar use and benefitt and at (her) only disposall...with which the...Earl of Exeter should not intermedle and nor should the same in any sort be lyable to his debts, Arts or Disposition.' And the Exeters did indeed look after them: Horace Walpole visited Burghley House in July 1763 and noticed a 'shrine full of crystal vases, filigree, enamels and the trinkets of taste that have belonged to many a noble dame'. The sixteenth-century narrative jewels in the collection illustrate episodes from the Bible and from classical antiquity. According to a schedule of 1690 a pendent horse with jewelled trappings was ridden by a diminutive Cupid (now missing), thus transforming it into an allegory of the all-conquering power of love: 'A Cupid on horseback in gold enamelled with a gold chaine sett with rubies and diamonds and three pendent pearls'. The motif of Cupid victorious on horseback alludes to the Asiatic conquests of Alexander the Great astride his celebrated horse, Bucephalus (Plate 12). A scene from Ovid's *Metamorphoses* is enacted in a small 'Round openwork plate of gold Enamel'd in little the story of Actaeon'. It depicts the cruel punishment of the huntsman Actaeon, who having inadvertently witnessed Diana and her nymphs bathing was transformed into a stag and torn to pieces by his own pack of hounds. The small figure of Cupid squats underneath this violent tableau, flanked by his bow and quiver (Plate 13). The Bible is the source of two miracles represented on the back and front of a locket cover: Elijah ascends to heaven in a chariot of fire while Elisha rends his

clothes beside the river Jordan, which Elijah's mantle has divided (Kings II, vv. 1-13) (Plate 14) and on the reverse Jonah, disgorged by a huge fish onto dry land (Jonah III v. 10) (Plate 15). Bright with translucent green, red, blue and yellow enamels, these scenes shine out like the panels of stained glass windows.

Plate 12 (*top*). Prancing horse pendant, originally ridden by Cupid.

Plate 13 (*above*). The punishment of Actaeon, who was turned into a stag and torn to pieces by his hounds for inadvertently surprising Diana and her nymphs bathing.

Plate 14 (*top*). Shell locket cover depicting the ascent of Elijah to heaven in a chariot of fire.

Plate 15 (*above*). The inside of the shell locket cover depicting Jonah emerging from the jaws of the whale.

The Penruddock Jewel

Narrative jewels are of small intrinsic value, which accounts for their survival. Those set with valuable stones – the gorgeous collars, girdles, necklaces, headbands, bracelets and pendants seen in sixteenth-century portraits (Plate 2) – were inevitably broken up either to raise money or for resetting. Only one jewel designed round a valuable gemstone remains in the family of the original owner, Sir George Penruddock, soldier and Member of Parliament for Wiltshire in the 1560s. It is a pendent triangle with a large cabochon sapphire in the centre framed in rubies and diamonds. Queen Katherine Parr gave it to Sir George who wears it on a gold chain in his portrait by Lucas de Heere. The Penruddocks of Compton Chamberlayne were loyal to King Charles I and when beseiged by Cromwell's soldiers during the Civil War they threw their ancestral jewel into the lake in front of the house rather than let it fall into Parliamentarian hands. The chain was lost but the pendant recovered. It was last shown at the exhibition of the Royal House of Tudor, held in 1890.

Accessories

The skills of the Renaissance goldsmith transformed everyday useful objects into fine jewels. Pomanders – made of aromatic substances such as cloves, cinnamon, musk, ambergris and civet rolled into balls – were either caged or netted in gold and silver or carried in decorative containers to scent the foul air and protect from infection. It is known that John Mabbe, a London jeweller, had two hundred and twenty pomanders in his stock in 1576, and although they were obviously widely used at that time few have survived. There is one in the British Museum which was fished out of the Thames in 1854, but it is no more than a skeleton of gold wire, devoid of embellishment. Another, which happily is very well preserved, is at Burghley House. This splendid pomander is pear-shaped, while the pattern of brightly coloured open scrolls allows the aromatic substances to be enjoyed when pressed to the nose (Plate 16). Like prayer books, these containers usually hung from a long chain at the girdle.

Plate 16. An enamelled gold pomander containing aromatic
substances to sweeten the air.

Picks for the teeth and ears were carried in imaginatively designed cases such as the pistol-shaped étui with snake entwined round the handle said to have belonged to Anne Boleyn, who used the pistol as a whistle to summon her servants or hounds. On the morning of her execution she gave it to Captain Gwyn, Officer of the Guard, saying it was the first token which the King had given her and that, just as the serpent was part of the design, so 'a serpent the giver had proved to her'. It is on loan to the Victoria and Albert Museum.

Magical Jewels

The longstanding belief in the magical powers of certain substances and inscriptions was not questioned by the Tudors. In about 1540 the Campion family of Danny in Sussex had a piece of unicorn horn – in reality narwhal tusk – mounted in a gold boat-shaped pendant ornamented with black and white interlaced lines. As the unicorn always – according to legend – assayed drinking water by dipping his horn in it, so it was thought that a piece of its horn would detect poison. The Danny jewel was given to the Victoria and Albert Museum in 1917. Another lucky substance, which people believed would protect the wearer from drowning, was taken from babies born within the caul, that is with part of the membrane which encloses the foetus still covering the head. When Sir John Monson, MP for Lincoln and ancestor of the present Lord Monson, was born in this way, a gold heart locket was made for his caul, inscribed JOHN MONSON BORN THE TENTH OF SEPTEMBER AT 12 OF THE CLOK AT NIGHT 1597. This is on loan to the Victoria and Albert Museum.

21

Scottish Jewellery

The Scots had a particularly strong belief in the magical powers of stones and wore them in brooches and lockets as a protection from misfortune at home and abroad. One jewel which proved efficacious is listed in the 1640 inventory of Sir Colin Campbell of Glenorchy: 'Ane stone of the quantity of half ane hen's egg set in silver being flat at the ane end and round at the other like ane peire [pear]. Sir Colin Campbell first Laird of Glenurqhy wore [it] when he fought in the Battell at Rhodes against the Turks he being of the knights of Rhodes'.

In some old Scottish families the traditional brooch which fastened the plaid across the shoulder, from where it fell in graceful folds, was proudly brought out for visitors who were told its full history. Thomas Pennant in Banffshire recalled being shown in 1769 'a very ancient brotche which the Highlanders use like the fibula of the Romans to fasten their vest', by Colonel Campbell of Glenlyon. Pearls, amethysts and crystals in high turrets embellish this wide — 3-inch diameter — silver gilt ring, and the back is inscribed with the names CASPAR MELCHIOR BALTAZAR, the three Magi who protected against epilepsy, and CONSUMATUM, the last word of Christ on the cross, another powerful talisman. This was sold at Christie's on 21 May 1897 and is now in the British Museum, along with a silver brooch from Lochbuy. The centre of the Lochbuy brooch is filled with a domed crystal — which has a cavity for a relic inside — encircled by river pearls in tall turrets with filigree between. An inscription in eighteenth-century script on the back tells its story:

The silver oar of this brooch was found on the estate of Loch Buy in Mull and made by a tinker on that estate about the year 1500. It was handed down by the ladies of that family to one another until Anna Campbell Lady to Murdock Maclean who had no male issue gave it to Isabella Maclean their daughter spouse to John Scrogie to whom she presented it the day after their marriage.

While on a visit to Scotland in 1847 Mrs George Bancroft, wife of the American ambassador, being near Oban, 'wished much to see the ruins of Dunolly. We passed the porter's lodge and found ourselves directly in the most picturesque grounds on the very shore of the ocean with the Western Isles lying before us...we went into the house...and to my great delight Captain Macdougal brought out the great brooch of Lorn which his ancestor won from Bruce and the Story of which you will find in the *Lord of the Isles*'.

Although the brooch is no longer kept at Dunolly Castle it remains in the possession of the Clan Macdougall, whose Chief, Madam MacDougall, has written an account of its history:

The Brooch of Lorne is a reliquary brooch of continental origin. It has been suggested that the central crystal might have been brought from the Crusades. Tradition has it that the Brooch was captured from King Robert the Bruce at the Battle of Dalry in 1306 by the MacDougalls of Lorne. When fleeing from the battle three MacDougall clansmen sprang on his horse: he killed them, but one of the three still held the King's cloak in his grasp. The King unclasped the Brooch which was holding the cloak and it fell to the ground and was captured by the MacDougalls. Bruce and the MacDougalls were on opposite sides because Bruce had murdered the Red Comyn who was related to the MacDougall chief by marriage.

In the Covenanting Wars the Brooch was looted during the sack and burning of the MacDougall Castle of Gylen on the island of Kerrera. It remained in the possession of the Campbells of Bargleann and was found in the charter chest when the Campbell of that day died. It was agreed by the trustees, Campbell of Lochnell, the widow and two other trustees it should be returned to the MacDougall chief, and Captain John MacDougall received the brooch on behalf of his father in 1822.

Captain John MacDougall of MacDougall was present during the visit of Queen Victoria and the Prince Consort to Lord Breadalbane at Taymouth Castle in 1842. John was asked to steer the Queen's barge for her trip on Loch Tay and when he was presented to the Queen Lord Breadalbane mentioned the brooch was once worn by Bruce. The Queen looked at the brooch and when she returned it asked the name of the centre stone. Family tradition has it that John felt the Queen expected him to beg her to accept the brooch but in spite of his fervent loyalty thus far he refused to go.

Plate 17 (*right*). The gold rosary which Queen Mary Stuart carried to her execution in 1587.

Plate 18 (*far right*). Portrait of Mrs Henry Howard of Corby wearing the Queen Mary Stuart rosary as a necklace.

Mary Stuart

In Scotland relics of their royal house were cherished by the great families such as the Campbells of Glenorchy. Among their jewels listed in 1640 was a brooch given by King James V (1512-42): 'ane targett of gold sett with thrie diamondis four topaces or jacints ane rubie and ane saphyre enambled given be [by] King James the Fyt [Fifth] of worthie memorie to ane Laird of Glenurqhey his predicessours'. The most numerous and the most poignant of Scottish royal mementos are those associated with the tragic life of Queen Mary, executed at Fotheringay Castle in 1587: some were keepsakes for friends, others were acquired many years later by those devoted to her memory, for she cast a spell in death no less than in life. During the long years of imprisonment following her escape from Scotland in 1567, Queen Mary took to wearing devotional jewellery with her widow's weeds in affirmation of her position as martyr for the persecuted Catholic faith. There is a gold crucifix — signifying her belief that through the Cross true faith would ultimately triumph — in the Duke of Norfolk's

collection at Arundel Castle, which was sold in 1696 to Lady Mary Howard, wife of Lord Thomas Howard Master of the Robes to James II, by the Benedictine monk Father Lowick. He said that Queen Mary had given the crucifix to John Feckenham, the last Abbot of Westminster, who like her had endured many years in prison.

Queen Mary went to her death with great dignity, and her stately appearance made an unforgettable impression. She wore a black dress over a red petticoat, a white cap and a transparent veil falling over her shoulders down to her hem. One of her little dogs was hidden beneath her gown, a touching symbol of fidelity. Before she died she affirmed her faith: 'I am settled in the ancient Catholic Roman religion and mind to spend my blood in it.' In token of this she carried an enamelled gold rosary, bequeathed in her will to Anne Dacre, daughter-in-law of the fourth Duke of Norfolk. The black, white and blue beads terminate in a crucifix, at the back of which the Virgin of the Immaculate Conception stands upon a crescent moon (Plate 17). From Anne Dacre — who had been extremely helpful in replenishing the

Queen's wardrobe — the rosary descended to the eleventh Duke of Norfolk who gave it to the antiquary, Henry Howard of Corby, himself a descendant of Anne Dacre's sister Elizabeth, wife of Lord 'Belted Will' Howard. In a portrait painted in about 1830 Mrs Henry Howard wears the rosary like a necklace, thereby asserting her pride in its historical and religious importance (Plate 18). During the lifetime of the fifteenth Duke of Norfolk (1847-1917) it was returned to Arundel. There are several other rosaries said to have belonged to Queen Mary. That lent by the Earl of Northesk to the exhibition of the Royal House of Stuart in 1889 was inherited from Mary Beaton, one of her ladies in waiting. The carved wood beads with relic of the True Cross attached, which were a gift to her friend Sir William Herbert, are still at Powis Castle. The Berington rosary at Little Malvern Court, Worcester, could be Spanish. The Paters (for reciting the Our Father) are jet, carved on one side with Christ crowned with thorns, and on the other with the head of St James of Compostella, whose badge, the cockleshell, is repeated again in the jet Aves (for saying the Hail Mary) which alternate with ebony beads: all the beads are strung on silver chains.

An equally religious relic of Mary Stuart is the double-sided bloodstone cameo of the Crucifixion and the Flagellation, enclosed in an agate egg which is still, with other important Stuart relics, in the collection of the family of the Scottish nobleman to whom she gave them. It is now worn as a pendant to an eighteenth-century bloodstone bead necklace (Plate 19).

And cameos survive as secular mementos of Queen Mary too, for just as Queen Elizabeth gave her cameo portrait to her closest supporters, so did she. On becoming engaged to the fourth Duke of Norfolk — an event which led to his own execution on suspicion of treason in 1572 — she sent him her cameo portrait framed in golden leaves studded with turquoises, rubies and emeralds and hung with three pearls. In the eighteenth century it was acquired from the Arundel collection by the Earl of Oxford, who left it to his daughter the Duchess of Portland: it has been at Welbeck Abbey ever since. There is another cameo portrait, set in a heart-shaped mount, among the Penicuik jewels said to have been gifts to Gillis Mowbray, her maid of honour at Fotheringay. The other relics are a locket with miniatures of Queen Mary and her small son, the future James VI of Scotland and James I of England, a black and white pearl pendant, and a necklace of fourteen large beads probably made from a pair of pomander bracelets. In 1923 the Clerks of Penicuik in Lothian sent them for auction in Edinburgh where they were bought for the Royal Museum of Scotland.

The necklace of twenty-nine pearls of 'unusually fine colour' said to have been presented by Queen Mary to Elizabeth Neville, wife of the Henry Lord Abergavenny who was one of the peers officiating at the Fotheringay trial of 1586, was sold by her descendant, the Marquess of Abergavenny, at Christie's on 4 June 1849. But another of Queen Mary's necklaces is at Arundel Castle, for it was bought as a wedding present for his wife Lady Flora Hastings by the fifteenth Duke of Norfolk in 1877, who believed Queen Mary sent it as a love token to his ancestor the fourth Duke of Norfolk on their engagement. The thirty-four pearls are mounted in gold collets with fleurs-de-lis spacers between (Plate 20). The

Plate 19 (*above*). Agate locket enclosing a bloodstone cameo of the Crucifixion: the Flagellation is engraved on the back.

Plate 20 (*right*). Pearl and gold fleur-de-lis necklace, allegedly sent by Queen Mary Stuart to the fourth Duke of Norfolk on their engagement.

chain of ruby, emerald and pearl snakes given to the devoted lady in waiting Mary Seton was divided in the early seventeenth century. Part was brought in 1695 by her descendant, the Hon. Elizabeth Seton, to the Hay family of Duns Castle, who still own it, and the rest — sold with the Eglinton jewels at Christie's on 22 February 1894 — is now in the royal collection at Windsor Castle: it was given as a Silver Jubilee present by Countess Bathurst in 1935.

A pendant of Cupid firing his arrow standing tip-toe on a wounded heart inscribed WILLINGLY WOUND was a gift from Mary Stuart to George Gordon fourth Marquess of Huntly. And she gave another pendant of great quality to James Gordon of Methlick, ancestor of the Earls and Marquesses of Aberdeen. A white hand grips a laurel wreath enclosing a crystal reliquary containing a curl of Queen Mary's dark brown hair. The Gordons of Haddo remained loyal to the Stuarts until the accession of the third Earl in 1745 when they switched allegiance to the Hanoverians. In the nineteenth century Countess Mary, wife of the fifth Earl, recognising its historical and artistic significance, designated it an heirloom. Ever since it has been worn by the reigning Marchioness of Aberdeen (Plate 21).

Whereas these pendants remain in their original condition a sapphire from Queen Mary — now at Lennoxlove — was set in a ring ornamented with black and white acanthus leaves in the late seventeenth century (Plate 22). The back was inscribed: SENT BY QUEEN MARY OF SCOTLAND AT HER DEATH TO JOHN MARQUIS OF HAMILTON (Plate 23). Another relic of Queen Mary is a ring once owned the Earl of Ilchester: its bezel is a ruby cameo death's head with diamond eyes; beneath are enamelled crossbones.

Plate 22. Sapphire sent by Queen Mary to the Marquis of Hamilton, set in a seventeenth-century ring.

Plate 21 (*left*). Jewelled gold pendent hand grasping a laurel wreath flanked by dragons emerging from cornucopiae framing a crystal reliquary containing a curl of Queen Mary's hair: Queen Mary gave it to James Gordon of Methlick in Aberdeenshire.

Plate 23. The back of the Queen Mary ring, with its inscription.

Devotional Jewels

Queen Mary's adherence to her faith attracted the support of the leading Roman Catholics in Scotland and England, who were known as Recusants — that is Catholics who refused to conform to the state church and made an open and explicit refusal by not attending their parish church. They suffered for this by being continually fined or sentenced to periodic imprisonment, and a number of devotional jewels made for and used by them have survived in their families. The earliest is the gold rosary which the Victoria and Albert Museum bought in 1934 from the Langdales of Houghton Hall in Yorkshire, who had found it in a box of oddments. The facets of the fifty small Aves, and the six larger lozenge-shaped Paters, and the terminating melon-shaped pendant are all engraved with saints, identified by inscriptions. These images are identical with those on a distinctive type of devotional finger ring found only in Scotland and England, and which were named 'iconographic' by Victorian collectors. The rosary must therefore be of British and not foreign manufacture. All the beads date from about 1500, except for two which depict Saints William of Norwich, William of Rochester and Edelient of Cornwall, which therefore suggest that the owner was a Langdale ancestor, the Recusant Lord William Howard (1563-1640), friend and patron of the Cornish scholar Nicholas Roscarrock, author of the life of Saint Edelient. Lord William, the 'Belted Will Howard' of Sir Walter Scott's romantic poem, *The Lay of the Last Minstrel*, was the son of the fourth Duke of Norfolk and husband of Elizabeth Dacre, a great heiress. Their idyllic and patriarchal existence at Naworth Castle in Cumberland collecting books, works of art and antiquities amidst a crowd of children and grandchildren was described in a Survey of the North compiled in 1634: 'the noble twain as it pleased themselves to tell us themselves could not make above twenty five years together when first they married but now could make above one hundred and forty years and are hearty, well and merry'.

Devotional jewellery which belonged to the Lord Chancellor and saint, Sir Thomas More (1478-1535) — a silver seal, a cameo of the Virgin, a large

reliquary and two crucifixes — was kept for over two centuries by his Recusant descendants at Barnborough Hall in Yorkshire. Then in 1755, Father Thomas More, S.J., who described himself as 'the last of the family of Sir Thomas More', gave them to the Society of Jesus, and in 1794 they were sent to Stonyhurst College in Lancashire where they have since remained. The larger of the gold crucifixes, hung with pearls, once contained a relic of Sir Thomas's patron saint for it has a Greek inscription translating, 'This is a relic of the Apostle Thomas'. The front of the round pendent reliquary is embossed with St George and the Dragon, and the back with a complex group: Christ seated on the tomb with the Instruments of the Passion with the heads of those who betrayed Him — Caiaphas, Judas, Peter and the maidservant. Around the sides — interspersed with pansies — an inscription alludes to the ordeal endured in the months leading up to his execution: O PASSI GRAVIORA DABIT [DEUS] HIS QUOQUE FINEM (O friends, that have endured yet heavier blows [God] will grant an ending to them). This statement of faith from Virgil's *Aeneid* reflects the humanist philosophy of Sir Thomas More who was a brilliant classical scholar as well as an ardent Catholic.

Rings

In Shakespeare's *All's Well That Ends Well* (Act III, Scene 7), Helena speaks of her husband's family ring:

> ...a ring the county wears,
> That downward hath succeeded in his house
> From son to son, some four or five descents
> Since the first father wore it: this ring he holds
> In most rich choice;

Helena's words could apply equally to the gold signet still worn by Lord Mowbray and Stourton which belonged to a famous Tudor ancestor, Sir Edward Howard (1476-1513), standard bearer to King Henry VIII, and Lord High Admiral from 1512 until he was killed during a sea battle with the French in 1513. He died like a hero: 'Thus fell one of the bravest of the brave, rashly indeed, yet in unison with his professed feeling and principle that the

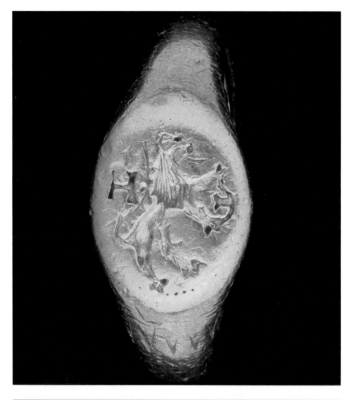

valour of a seaman ought to approach to madness' (Plate 24).

A very different character from the impetuous and gallant Sir Edward is evoked by a signet at Chatsworth dated 1588, engraved with the arms of Richard Boyle (1566-1643) (Plate 25). It was a farewell present from his mother when he left England for Ireland at the age of twenty-two with no other assets save this ring, his legal training, fine clothes, rapier, dagger, bracelet, a small diamond ring and £27 in his pocket. An astute businessman, he took advantage of every opportunity that presented itself and rose from the ranks of minor officialdom to become Lord High Treasurer of Ireland and the 'great Earl of Cork', ancestor of Richard fourth Earl of Cork and third Earl of Burlington, patron of the arts and father of Charlotte Boyle who was to marry the fourth Duke of Devonshire.

There are two other crystal signets in ancestral collections, but neither is heraldic. One at Burghley House is engraved with two crowned shields emblazoned with forget-me-nots and inscribed with the sacred monogram, IHC — the abbreviated Greek form of the name of Jesus — and also FGMN, the initials of the word forget-me-not (Plate 26). The other, at Grimsthorpe Castle in Lincolnshire, represents a pair of clasped hands holding a heart and bears the date 1585. It is likely to have belonged to Peregrine Bertie, twelfth Baron Willoughby De Eresby. A year later, in 1586, he joined the British army in Flanders commanded by the Earl of Leicester. As one of the best swordsmen in England he is the hero of the old ballad 'The Brave Lord Willoughby':

> The fifteenth day of July
> With glistering spear and shield
> A famous fight in Flanders
> Was foughten in the field.
> The most courageous officers
> Were English captains three,
> But the bravest man in battle
> Was brave Lord Willoughby.

Disliking the obsequiousness of Elizabethan court life, the Baron remained abroad and in 1589 took command of the English forces supporting Henry of Navarre, and there endured great privations until he

Plate 24 (*top*). Gold signet with blanch lion and initials EH, for Sir Edward Howard, Lord High Admiral of England, killed in battle in 1513.

Plate 25 (*above*). Gold signet set with rock crystal, with the arms of Robert Boyle, first Earl of Cork. The back is inscribed BOYLE 1588.

Plate 26. Gold betrothal signet set with rock crystal engraved with twin shields: one bears the monogram of Christ, IHC, the other a spray of forget-me-nots.

Plate 27. Gold, mother-of-pearl and ruby locket ring with diamonds forming the letters E(lizabeth) and R(egina) in blue enamel.

Plate 28. The inside of the locket seen in Plate 27, showing busts of Queen Elizabeth and her mother Anne Boleyn, wearing brooches set with a ruby and a diamond.

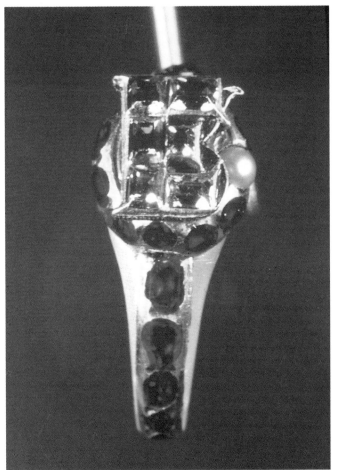

returned home in January 1590. His services were acknowledged by two royal gifts: an emerald intaglio portrait of King Henry and a large diamond which was later recut as a brilliant and mounted in a gold rim inscribed DIAMOND GIVEN BY HENRY IV. Both these mementos are also still at Grimsthorpe Castle.

According to the catalogue of a sale held at Christie's on 26 February 1879, a signet set with a very large ruby engraved with the crowned monogram of King Henry VIII came from 'an old mansion in Scotland'. This has disappeared. But, fortunately, the royal locket ring of mother-of-pearl sold by the Earl of Home at Christie's on 17 June 1920 is still in England where it is displayed at Chequers, the Prime Minister's country residence, one of the many gifts from Viscount Lee of Fareham when he presented that house to the nation. The bezel, which is set with diamonds forming the monogram E, with R in blue enamel (Plate 27), lifts up to show two miniature busts of Queen Elizabeth and her mother Anne Boleyn, wearing a diamond and a ruby brooch respectively (Plate 28). The Queen's emblem of the phoenix rising from a flaming crown is on the back of the bezel. Rubies encircle the sides of the bezel and stud the shoulders. According to tradition this little masterpiece of English jewellery was a gift from James I to the first Lord Home who accompanied him from Scotland to England on his accession in 1603.

Two
THE STUARTS

James I

A 'blue ring from a fair lady' summoned King James south to claim the crown of England. On 24 March 1603, as Queen Elizabeth lay dying, Philadelphia Lady Scrope, daughter of Henry first Lord Hunsdon, dropped a star-shaped diamond and sapphire ring from the window of St James's Palace to her young brother Robert who was waiting below, ready to mount his horse. She pointed northwards, and he rode hard to Scotland with the ring in his pocket. James, who had been waiting for this signal — prearranged with Lady Scrope — that the time had come for him to claim his English inheritance, set out for London immediately. He kept the ring as a token of the event which had transformed the fortunes of his family and his grandson, King James II, gave it to the Duchess of Buckingham, his daughter by Catherine Sedley. More Stuart than the Stuarts themselves, her pride in her royal descent and contempt for the lower orders was extreme: outraged by the preaching of the evangelist George Whitefield, she complained to the devout Countess of Huntingdon, 'It is monstrous to be told that you have a heart as sinful as the common wretches that crawl the earth. I cannot but wonder that your ladyship should relish any sentiments so much at variance with high rank and good breeding.' She did, however, approve of John Earl of Orrery to whom she left the ring and

he certainly appreciated this 'most noble legacy left me, whose great value, sett in diamonds whose lustre borrow brightness from the stone they surround'. His descendants sent it to the exhibition at the Victoria and Albert Museum in 1872: it has not been publicly shown since.

Both King James and his wife Queen Anne spent prodigiously on jewels and surrounded themselves with those who did likewise. This was partly a reaction to the austere life in Edinburgh at Holyroodhouse, but it had a political purpose too, for believing as he did in the divine right of kings, King James must have felt the need to assert his elevated status with a show of outward magnificence.

He appointed a Master of Ceremonies to distribute his presents to foreign diplomats, to escort them on presentation and departure from court and to decide on all questions of protocol. To preserve this expertise acquired by long experience, the office became hereditary, passing from Sir Charles Cottrell, appointed in 1641, to his descendants well into the reign of George III. On the eve of his coronation in 1661 Charles II gave Sir Charles Cottrell a new badge which is still in the family collection at Rousham House in Oxfordshire. Crowned and framed in diamonds, it bears two mottoes of James I: on the front the biblical phrase BEATI PACIFICI (Blessed are the peacemakers) with a hand holding out an olive branch, emblematic of peace, and on the back the royal motto

Plates 29 and 30. Pendent miniature of Queen Mary of Modena, wife of King James II, crowned with three rose-cut diamonds, with royal cipher J(acobus) M(aria) R(egentes) at the back.

DIEU ET MON DROIT (God and my right) with a gauntleted arm brandishing a sword to punish and protect. Worn from a gold chain, this badge appears in the portraits of successive Masters at Rousham (Plates 31 and 32).

The value of the jewels given to foreign diplomats reflected the glory of the Stuart monarchy, and James was equally generous to his own subjects. Those given to Sir Duncane Campbell were recorded in 1640: 'ane rounde jewell of gold sett with precious stones conteining twentie nyne diamonds and four great rubies quhilk [which] Queen Anna of worthie memorie Queen of Great Britane France and Irland gave to...Sir Duncane Campbell of Glenourqhy. Item ane gold ring sett with ane great diamond scahpine [shaped] lyke a heart and uther four small diamonds quilk [which] the said Queen Anna of worthie memorie gave to the said Sir Duncane.'

At Holkham Hall, the great Palladian house which dominates the marshes of northern Norfolk, there was for many years a ring which Queen Anne gave the eminent lawyer Sir Edward Coke for his part in bringing the King's favourite, Robert Carr, to trial for the murder of Sir Thomas Overbury. It was 'set with a great diamond cut with fawcetts' − that is rose-cut, a method of faceting which released more light from the stone than the early point and table cuts. Preserved with it was Sir Edward's collar of SS, the insignia he wore as Lord Chief Justice. He was so proud of this office that when he was replaced in 1616 Sir Edward refused to relinquish the collar to his successor − as was customary − and insisted instead that it should remain at Holkham for 'his posterity that they might one day know they had a Chief Justice to their ancestor'. Sadly, these mementos of royal regard and professional distinction have vanished, as has Queen Anne's splendid dynastic collar of Tudor roses given after her death in 1618 by King James to the Duchess of Richmond and Lennox, wife of his cousin, Ludovic Stuart. This haughty Duchess lived in great state at Exeter House in the Strand, and when painted by William Larkin she wore the collar to emphasise her close family relationship with royalty. She bequeathed it to her husband's nephew James in 1639 with the words: 'my great collar of red and white roses of diamonds and rubies usually

Plate 31 (*top*). Sir Clement Cottrell, Master of Ceremonies, wearing his badge presented by King Charles II.

Plate 32 (*above*). Sir Clement Cottrell-Dormer, Master of Ceremonies to King George II, wearing the same badge.

called Lancaster and York which blessed King James gave me'. It survived the Civil War and was last mentioned in an indenture of 1667 between the Dowager Duchess of Richmond and Lennox and Humphrey Wold, this time described as 'One cheyne called York and Lancaster consisting of two and thirty links of roses set round with diamonds rubyes and a faire table diamond in the midst'.

As had been Queen Elizabeth's custom, King James and Queen Anne acknowledged loyal service with gifts of portraits. Those that survived are miniatures, of which two — the Lyte and Eglinton jewels — remained in the families of the original owners for centuries. The Queen's miniature by Nicholas Hilliard in a red enamelled case — most probably made by the court jeweller George Heriot — with her diamond monogram and two SS (perhaps for Sovereign) hangs from a ribbon over the breast of Lady Ann Liviston in a portrait in the Seafield collection in Scotland. As a girl Lady Ann entered the Queen's service, in return for the promise that she would receive a dowry and all her wedding expenses. This was never honoured, but in recompense the Queen gave her the miniature, and other jewels — a collar, a pair of bracelets, a pendant and a chain — on her marriage in 1612 to Sir Alexander Seton of Foulstruther, afterwards sixth Earl of Eglinton. Sold by Lady Ann's descendant the Earl of Eglinton at Christie's on 13 July 1922 for £997 10s, the miniature is now in the Fitzwilliam Museum, Cambridge.

King James gave his miniature — also by Nicholas Hilliard — to Mr Lyte of Lytes Cary in Somerset in 1610 as a reward for his feat in tracing the royal pedigree back to Brut, a refugee from Troy and mythical founder of the British nation. The openwork cover which bears the royal monogram IR (Jacobus Rex) is liberally studded with table and rose-cut diamonds and the back is enamelled with red and blue broken scrollwork on a white ground. Thomas Lyte had his portrait painted wearing the miniature hanging from a red ribbon, and with the jewel it passed from eldest son to eldest son until 1747, when Thomas Lyte — a great-great-grandson — left them to the female line: 'my will and desire is that the said jewell and my great grandfather's picture may after my said daughter's death go and remain for the use of her

daughters successively and their respective issue'. In the nineteenth century Mrs Laura Dunn Monypenny sold the miniature to 'a stranger' and it was then bought through a London dealer by the Duke of Hamilton. Baron Ferdinand de Rothschild paid £2,835 for it at the Hamilton Palace sale of 1882, and left it to the British Museum with the Waddesdon Bequest in 1898.

A fine book-shaped pomander in the Pennington-Mellor-Munthe collection is close in style to the Lyte jewel: the openwork covers are composed of broken scrollwork, soberly enamelled in black, blue and white and enlivened by diamonds at the corners and centre. The design is neat and practical, for although the book does not open on hinges the pomander can be replaced by removing the bottom panel which slides out ingeniously (Plate 33). The pomander belonged to Philadelphia, wife of Thomas Wharton, and daughter of Robert first Earl of Monmouth, who had brought the news of Queen Elizabeth's death to King James in Scotland. Her brother-in-law

Plate 33. Jewelled book pomander. The bottom slides out so that the aromatics can be replaced.

George Wharton is commemorated by a monogram jewel in the same collection composed of the letters GW enamelled white and black respectively, the G being set with table-cut rubies. The white memento mori – skull, crossbones and Maltese cross – hanging below recall George's death in 1609 at the age of twenty-eight in a duel with Sir James Stewart of Blantyre whom he had accused of cheating at cards. Both these hot-tempered young blades were killed and were buried in anonymous graves at Highbury. Years after the tragedy, when the two families were reconciled, George Wharton's rapier was returned to his relations who put it on display with gifts of the royal Stewart plaid and a Van Dyck portrait of James Stewart, posthumous son of the dead duellist, all of which are still at Southside House (Plate 34).

Three more Jacobean jewels whose provenance has been authenticated are decorated with the characteristic broken scrollwork, enamelled black. Two are designed as weapons, redolent of authority and valour. One, an étui containing picks for teeth and ears, is a miniature version of the intricate wheel-lock pistols carried by the nobility: the distinctive curved line of the butt and the terminal of the dog-spring are all accurately rendered, albeit on a very small scale. Somewhat damaged by fire, it was acquired by the Victoria and Albert Museum in 1922 from the Pasfield family of Rotherhithe and Barbados. The 1690 Burghley schedule lists the second, 'a little Cymeter sett with turquoise and part of the Chaine to it', and a row of bright blue turquoises studding the scabbard emphasise the oriental character of this Hungarian pendent scimitar, perhaps also used as a pick (Plate 35). The third jewel, known as the Barrington cross, is set with six white table-cut diamonds – foiled black – around a rich yellow diamond and hung with two pearls. It was sold at Sotheby's on 25 June 1959 by the Hon. Rupert Barrington, who had inherited at from the Hon. Mrs James Anstruther, daughter-in-law of the fifth Viscount Barrington (Plates 36 and 37).

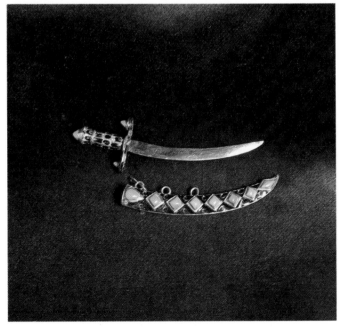

Plate 34 (*top*). Pendent cipher G(eorge) W(Harton). The Maltese cross and skull with crossbones refer to his death in a duel.

Plate 35 (*right*). Miniature pendent Hungarian scimitar set in the oriental style with turquoises.

Plate 36. The Barrington cross set with six white and one yellow Golconda diamonds.

Plate 37. The back of the Barrington cross, enamelled black with gold scrollwork.

Charles I

Jacobean jewellery is rare, but even less survives from the reign of Charles I, which was beset by political crises and civil war. For this reason the locket containing the miniature by David des Granges of the Royalist hero, Sir Bevil Grenville, is of particular interest, for it shows how superb the best Carolean craftsmanship was. The dense overall pattern of flowers enamelled on the front cover is studded with rubies, opals, diamonds and emeralds around a large sapphire: there is a bright geometric pattern on the back. Sir Bevil was killed at Lansdowne, near Bath, in

1643 and the locket passed to the Prideaux family and then to the Chichesters of Hall in Devonshire. The present head of the family, Major Charles Chichester, remembers his grandmother – who always wore the locket to the Bideford Horseshow Ball – lamenting its loss to her children. In about 1890 her husband had received a letter from Queen Victoria saying how pleased she would be if Mr Chichester would sell his locket to her great friend, Mr Ferdinand de Rothschild; obeying the royal command, Mr Chichester accepted £1,000 for it and it is now in the British Museum as part of the Waddesdon Bequest.

Plate 38. Dragonfly studded with cabochon rubies, garnets, opals and diamonds. The Countess of Exeter wore this in her hair.

Plate 39. The reverse of the Countess of Exeter's dragonfly jewel.

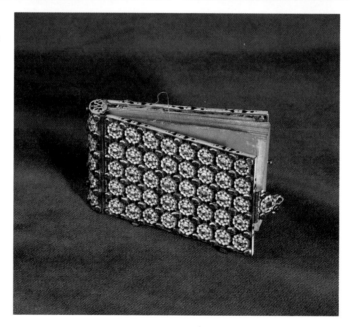

Plate 40. Jewelled girdle book, the covers decorated with Tudor roses each set with a table-cut diamond, with rubies between.

Two fine jewels from this period are mentioned in the 1690 Schedule at Burghley House: 'One Table Booke Enamel'd sett with Diamonds and Rubies inside', and a 'Lesser ffly sett with diamonds Rubys Opalls and Catts Eys' (Plates 38 and 39). The dragonfly is the only survivor out of five insect jewels listed in the Schedule, which Countess Elizabeth would have pinned in her hair. Interestingly, it is close in style to the cache of mid-seventeenth-century jewellery (perhaps the stock of a local jeweller) known as the Cheapside Hoard because it was found there in 1912 and now in the Museum of London. Some of the jewels compare with the Burghley 'Table Booke', which is a Carolean version of the Tudor girdle prayer book, though the family always believed it belonged to Queen Elizabeth because of its quality and the dynastic symbolism of the Tudor roses on the covers (Plate 40).

Although watches were not reliable timekeepers they were great seventeenth-century status symbols and given elaborate gold and jewelled cases. The watch which the daughter of King James I, Queen Elizabeth of Bohemia, gave Sir Frederick Harcourt, a soldier who served in the Low Countries, is still in the Harcourt family. The movement, which is signed K...AX, has an oval case with openwork covers and dial and is bright with enamels. It is protected by a silver pair-case and the key and a miniature of a young woman are attached to it (Plates 41 and 42). A round watch at Grimsthorpe Castle illustrates the mid-century botanical style: the dial is enamelled with a tulip and a lily in full bloom, and the back of the case with a bouquet of mixed flowers standing out in relief in filigree cagework on a gold ground (Plate 43).

Plates 41 and 42 (*top left and left*). Enamelled gold watch given by Queen Elizabeth of Bohemia to Sir Frederick Harcourt. The key and a miniature hang from the chain.

Plate 43 (*above*). Gold watch with a lily and a tulip on the dial. Of mid-seventeenth century date, it is an heirloom from Grimsthorpe Castle.

Plate 44. Diamond ring given by King Charles I to Sir Nicholas
Kemeys on the field of battle during the Civil War.

King Charles I has the reputation of a great connoisseur and jewels which he is known to have worn are of immense interest. Treasured above all is the large pear pearl which hung from his ear when he was executed in 1649: this he left to his daughter Mary, the mother of King William III, who in turn gave it to the first Earl of Portland. It is kept at Welbeck Abbey with a note in the handwriting of Queen Mary II which reads: 'This pearle was taken out of the ye king my grandfather's ear after he was beheaded & given ye Princess Royall.' Mounted in an enamelled gold crown, it is now yellow with age.

Three rings which Charles I gave away have survived. A finely proportioned ring, enamelled blue and black and set with five diamonds in the form of a star, is in the Pennington-Mellor-Munthe collection (Plate 44). It dates from the Civil War; having invested Sir Nicholas Kemeys, who saved him from death on the battlefield, King Charles took the ring from his finger and gave it to his rescuer as an additional token of gratitude. In memory of this episode, thereafter the eldest son in each generation of Kemeys was christened Charles. Two other rings

recall the King's last moments. After making his confession to William Juxon, Bishop of London, King Charles gave him a ring set with his cornelian cameo portrait, wearing the laurel wreath and brooched cloak of a Roman emperor (Plate 45). Appointed Archbishop of Canterbury at the Restoration, Juxon returned this keepsake to King Charles II who entrusted it to the first Duke of St Albans, his son by Nell Gwynne. Another portrait ring, with his miniature framed in diamonds, was the King's last gift to the devoted Sir Henry Firebrace who also attended him on the scaffold. When Sir Henry's granddaughter Hester married the Earl of Denbigh in 1695 she brought this ring with her dowry and it is still in the family collection.

Silver portraits of King Charles seen in profile and wearing a deep lace collar — as portrayed by Antony Van Dyck — with the royal coat of arms at the back, were worn by Royalists. A very rubbed version is at Burghley House while another, in a later frame of diamonds, has been lent to the Victoria and Albert Museum by Lord O'Hagan. Those who responded to Queen Henrietta Maria's appeals for loans of

Plate 45. Gold ring with cornelian cameo portrait of King Charles I, wearing armour and wreathed like a Roman Emperor, a gift to his confessor, Bishop Juxon.

Plate 46. The back of the Charles I portrait ring, enamelled with classical acanthus ornament.

money were also given rings, lockets and bracelet slides bearing the royal portrait or monogram as pledges that they would be repaid once the monarchy was firmly established again. One of these tokens, a ring with rose-cut diamonds on the shoulders, set with a miniature of King Charles, was passed down for many generations by the Gresleys of Drakelow and only recently sold, still in its original presentation box, at Christie's on 25 November 1975.

After King Charles I's execution a whole series of heart-shaped pendants, rings with miniatures, symbols of sovereignty and mortality with commemorative inscriptions, were worn in memory of the royal martyr. A memorial miniature in a silver locket and a seal with royal portrait inscribed CAROLUS DG at Blair Castle in the collection of the Duke of Atholl are two of the few relics still in private ownership.

Gifts from Foreign Monarchs

Most of the massive gold chains and diamond rings given to Englishmen by foreign monarchs in gratitude for services were soon turned into cash, but there were exceptions. The great Earl of Cork was rich enough to keep and bequeath his son Richard, in the grandest terms, the gold chain and medallic portrait,

thereof which His Majesty of Denmark with his gracious letter sent unto me as a royal demonstration of his princely acceptance of my endeavours for preserving and supplying his great ship and men by that extraordinary tempests were put in at Youghal with express charges to my son never to part with it but as I had given it to him he was to leave it to his heirs to be forever continued to the House of the Earl of Cork, which house's unspotted honour and integrity I desire the Almighty for ever to uphold it with His Grace.

From Scotland, the courageous and cunning soldier Alexander first Earl of Leven (1580-1661) went to fight for King Gustavus Adolphus of Sweden who appointed him Field Marshal of his armies. In recognition of his services the King had medals struck in his honour and gave him his own seal. It is a garnet intaglio with the crowned monogram GAR (Gustavus Adolphus Rex) set in a ring in the eighteenth century, and it descended to Anna Maria, daughter of the eighth Earl of Leven and wife of Sir William Stirling Maxwell. She had a strong sense of history and gave it back to her cousin the ninth Earl, presenting it in a silver gilt box with a portrait of King Gustavus Adolphus and inscribed TO JOHN EARL OF LEVEN AND MELVILLE DEC 18 1870 FROM W & ASM. No longer in the Leven family, it is in a private London collection. Another Scottish family, the Campbells of Glenlyon, owned a jewel given to an ancestor by King Gustavus Adolphus's daughter the eccentric Queen Christina. This was sold by Christie's on 21 May 1897 and was described in the sale catalogue: 'formed as an expanded flower composed of nineteen petals of ovoid form each set with a table-cut diamond. The reverse of the jewel has a pierced floral border enriched with green, black, yellow and white enamel, and in the centre an oval locket with enamelled cover contains a gold medallion portrait of Queen Christina. The groundwork is enamelled light blue and the back of the medallion formed of a ducat of the arms of Sweden.'

Charles II

The Stuarts knew how to make gracious gestures and, in gratitude for their help in concealing him from the Parliamentarians in the Boscobel oak after the Battle of Worcester in 1651, the future King Charles II gave Richard Penderel and his brothers a yellow topaz, ruby and diamond ring which was a source of great pride to them. On his accession in 1660, King Charles rewarded Sir William Murray of Stanhope and Sir William Dugdale for their fidelity with memorial jewels of his father, and these were also treasured by successive generations. Nor did King Charles forget the memory of his great-grandmother Mary Queen of Scots, for he gave one of her rings to the first Duke of Grafton, his son by Barbara Villiers. This ring was inherited by Sir Almeric Fitzroy who served in the households of Queen Victoria and of King Edward VII and whose dark saturnine Stuart looks always amused the royal family. Sir Almeric had the pleasure of presenting this reminder of their common ancestress to Princess Mary when she married Viscount Lascelles in 1922; both

she and her mother Queen Mary must have been touched by his courtly gesture.

Stuart souvenirs can be found in the homes of other descendants of King Charles II by his various mistresses. The Duke of Cleveland — also a son by Barbara Villiers — inherited her medallic portrait of the King framed in rose diamonds, with the royal arms and inscription CAROLUS SECUNDUS at the back. It was sold by Christie's on 23 March 1938. At Goodwood House, Sussex seat of the Duke of Richmond and Gordon, there is a miniature of King Charles II in a diamond frame, and an emerald engraved with the entwined initials CL for Charles and Louise de Kéroualle — mother of the first Duke — crowned with ducal coronet and bordered with brilliant-cut diamonds, set in a ring. The fascinating group of jewels given to Nell Gwynne is owned by the Duke of St Albans: a diamond bodkin for her hair, with setting inscribed THE GIFT OF CHARLES 2ND TO NELLY GWYNNE (Plate 47); her diamond ring (Plate 48); and a memorial ring with the King's miniature and with a skull and the date of his death FEB 6 1684 CIIR on the back (Plates 49 and 50). Her large emerald, set in a gold buckle with roses in relief, is at Southside House. Sidney Beauclerk, grandson of the first Duke of St Albans, and Vice Chamberlain to King George II, gave it to his bride, Mary Morris of Speke Hall in Lancashire, and it descended to Mrs Hilda Pennington-Mellor-Munthe through the female line.

Plate 47 (*top left*). Nell Gwynne's diamond bodkin for her hair.

Plate 48 (*top right*). Diamond ring given by King Charles II to Nell Gwynne and preserved by her descendants.

Plate 49 (*right*). Memorial ring set with miniature of King Charles II, worn by the first Duke of St Albans.

Plate 50 (*far right*). The back of the memorial ring for King Charles II, inscribed with the royal initials CIIR and the date of death, FEB 6 1684, beneath a skull.

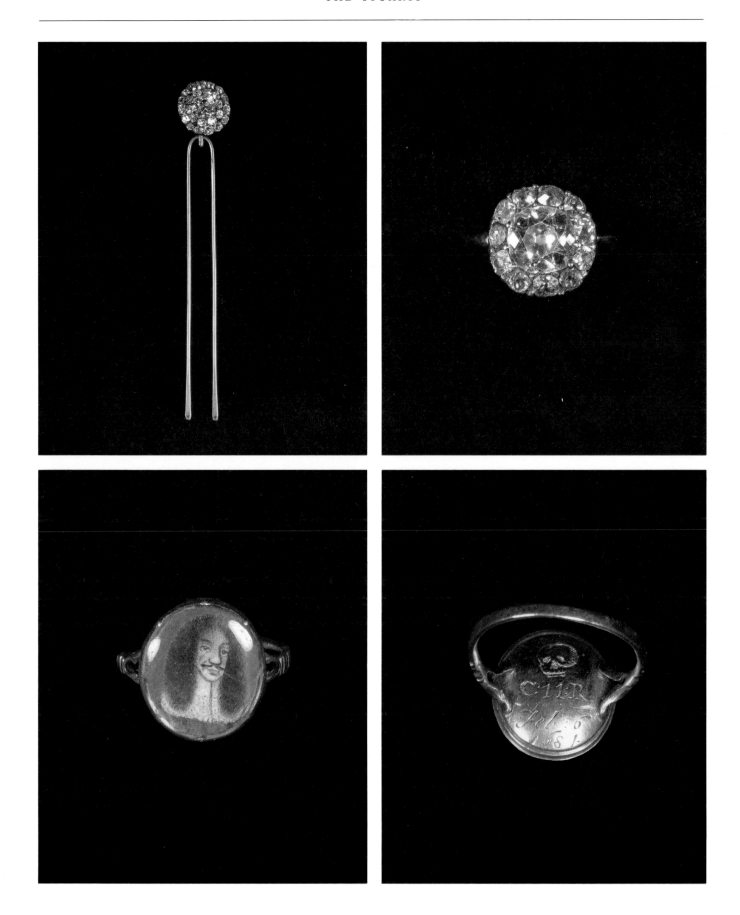

As godmother to Katherine, daughter of Thomas first Lord Clifford of Chudleigh (1630-73), Lord High Treasurer of England, Queen Katherine, wife of King Charles II, gave a present of a pair of diamond earrings which are still family heirlooms (Plate 51). Unfortunately, a diamond ring — also a gift from the Queen — mentioned in the wills of the second and third Lords Clifford has vanished. The Queen gave another pair of diamond earrings to Katherine Gregory (1679-1726), daughter of Sir William Gregory (1624-1696), Speaker of the House of Commons and Baron of the Exchequer, who was betrothed to Philip Hoskins in 1685: through this marriage these floral cluster earrings have descended to the Hornyold Stricklands of Sizergh Castle in Cumbria where they remain (Plate 52).

Plate 51. Earrings set with diamonds: a christening present to the Hon. Katherine Clifford from Queen Katherine in 1670.

James II

As the reign of James II was short and overshadowed by the political crisis which culminated in his exile of 1688 there are only a few jewels associated with him and with his second wife Queen Mary of Modena. The ruby chain ring — like a miniature bracelet — used at their wedding which took place at Dover in November 1673 is now at Arundel Castle. Although Queen Mary owned a diamond ring from the first proxy marriage in Modena, the ruby ring meant much more to her and as her most treasured possession she bequeathed it to her favourite nuns of the convent of the Visitation at Chaillot near Paris, from whom it came to the Dukes of Norfolk. The young Queen's miniature at Grimsthorpe Castle, set in a gold pendant crowned with three rose-cut diamonds, conveys her charm and good looks (Plate 29): the inscription at the back MARIA JACOBUS REGENTES dates from her short reign (Plate 30).

A few mementos of King James survive in the families of those who followed him into exile: a pair of square studs set with faceted crystal over the royal monogram JR and hair is at Sizergh Castle (Plate 53). The memorial brooch given to Sir Alexander Murray, MP for Peebles, with symbols of crown, cross-bones and skull, and inscribed JR OBIT SEPT. 16 1701 AETATIS 68, was lent by a descendant to the exhibition of the Royal House of Stuart in 1889.

Plate 52. Diamond cluster earrings given by Queen Katherine to Katherine Gregory.

Plate 53. Crystal memorial studs containing the hair of King James II with his cipher.

William and Mary

After Mary II died in 1694 her husband William III gave some of her jewels to their friends. A ruby and diamond ring, with a note in the Queen's handwriting, 'it was the first thing he ever did give me', and which she wore for her coronation in 1689, went to William Bentinck, first Earl of Portland, as did a pearl choker. When the sixth Duke of Portland married Miss Winifred Dallas-Yorke in 1889 she wore this large round pearl necklace with a pear drop pendant with her wedding dress, and was painted by Philip de László with it in her hand in 1912 (Plate 54). The Duchess brought to the collection at Welbeck Abbey

Plate 54. Winifred, wife of the sixth Duke of Portland, painted by Philip de László in 1912 with the pearl necklace of Queen Mary II. William III gave the necklace to the first Earl of Portland.

a hereditary jewel from her own family, a miniature case, studded with triangular diamonds in concentric rows with the back botanically enamelled on a white ground; it came from her ancestor James Dallas.

Although it is sometimes suggested that the marriage of King William III and Queen Mary II was unhappy, jewels associated with them contradict this. A pendant from their early married life was lent by Earl Spencer from the Althorp collection to the exhibition of jewellery held at the Birmingham City Art Gallery in 1960. Set with a large rose-cut diamond, it is enamelled at the back with their initials W and M beneath the royal crown of the Netherlands, and hangs from a ruby bow-knot inscribed with the affectionate declaration L'AMOUR EN EST LE LIEN (Love is our bond). King William gave the Queen's maid of honour Anne Grenville, granddaughter of the hero Sir Bevil Grenville, a jewel to wear in her memory, as he had done himself, tied to a ribbon round his arm. It holds a finely plaited lock of the Queen's hair, her monogram, and the symbols of death and sovereignty — crown, sceptre and orb — under rock crystal. The back is inscribed MEMENTO MARIA REGINA OBIT 28 DECEMBRIS 94. In 1872 Lady Llanover, a descendant, lent it to the jewellery exhibition at the Victoria and Albert Museum: it has not been exhibited since.

Garter Insignia

The most important surviving pieces of seventeenth-century jewellery are Garter insignia. The earliest — and a complete set — was made for the Earl of Northampton in 1629. His fortune came from his wife Elizabeth, daughter of the City merchant Sir John Spencer who had violently opposed the match. To escape from home she hid in a baker's basket and eloped with her lover: eventually her father forgave the couple and left them a vast inheritance which they thoroughly enjoyed spending. Lord Northampton rode to his installation as a Garter knight from his home, Salisbury House in the Strand, attended by a cortège of one hundred persons arrayed in such splendour that the chapter of the order gave him a special vote of thanks. His insignia consists of the blue velvet Garter with red and white motto, collar of twenty-six enamelled red roses within buckled Garters alternating with tasselled knots with pendent Great George liberally studded with diamonds, and a Lesser George – the badge of the order for everyday wear. These superb jewels remained in the Northampton family until 1980 when they were ceded to the British Museum in lieu of Capital Transfer Tax.

Another remarkable group of Garter insignia, this time dating from the second half of the century, remains in the collection of the Duke of Buccleuch.

A Lesser George which is said to have belonged either to General Monck first Duke of Albemarle, or to his son Christopher second Duke, could have come to the Buccleuchs through Ralph, future first Duke of Montagu, who married the mad widow of Duke Christopher in 1692 for her vast possessions. It is set both back and front with cameos of St George and the Dragon, and framed in large rose-cut diamonds, with a diamond over the suspension loop. A pendent George – worn from the collar at Garter ceremonies – perhaps part of the set given to the

Plate 55. Diamond-studded George from the Garter insignia of
the first Duke of Monmouth, given by his father King Charles II.

Duke of Monmouth by his father Charles II on his appointment to the order in 1663 is also in the Buccleuch collection, by direct descent, for the Duke of Monmouth married Anne Duchess of Buccleuch the same year (Plates 55 and 56). After leading the rebellion against his uncle James II in 1684, the Duke of Monmouth was defeated at Sedgmoor and found hiding in a ditch, disguised as a peasant. According to the diarist John Evelyn it was his George which gave him away, 'his beard being grown so long and so gray as hardly to be known had not his George discovered him which was found in his pocket'.

Another magnificent diamond-encrusted George was given by Queen Anne to the Duke of Marlborough on his appointment to the order in 1702. The Prince Regent acquired this historic jewel and in 1815 gave it to another victorious commander, the Duke of Wellington. Sir Winston Churchill wore it to the coronation of 1953, but it was stolen, on 9 December 1965 with other valuable insignia, from Apsley House which was by then part of the Victoria and Albert Museum (Plate 267).

Plate 56. The other side of the Duke of Monmouth's pendent George, showing the superb enamelling.

Pearls Beyond Price

When Cosimo, Grand Duke of Tuscany, visited England in 1669 he observed that English women liked pearls more than any other jewel, and wore them 'in necklaces of great price'. Thus they were valued higher even than diamonds, and in 1633 Henry Hawkins in *Partheneia Sacra* explained why:

If you would epitomise an ample estate and put the same into a little compendium with bias to carry your wealth about you, sell what you have and put it into a pearl. If you have anie suit in court it will purchase greater friends and procure you better preferment than the best deserts... it will make you more place in a throng of people of meer respect than a rushing whistler shall do torch in hand.

It is therefore understandable that a dispute over the Petre family pearls should turn out to be the cause of great bitterness, for these were prized beyond all their other possessions. In 1612 John Petre bequeathed his wife's pearl chain to their daughter-in-law Katherine, 'to be delivered within one month next after my death which I desire her to account of as poor notes of my affection nothing answerable to her great love, merit and desert towards me'. Katherine died in 1624, and in 1632 William Lord Petre gave the pearls − valued at £600, an enormous sum at the time − to Mary, wife of his son Robert. When she died in 1685 it was said that she had kept 'the Jewell in her closett neare 50 Yeares but did not shew it to any person now living neither can it be proved that she ever wore itt but that she frequently said she had a jewel which two of the Ladyes of the Family were pictured with wearing it about their breasts and in many Neccessities for many she used to say she had a Jewell which did belong to the family which would be the last thing in the World she would part with'. According to the evidence given by witnesses, on Lady Mary's death Thomas Lord Petre, being unmarried, took the necklace and carried it to Bridget, widow of his elder brother William, who had died in the Tower of London after being impeached on the false accusation of Titus Oates. He said, 'Sister, Lookeing over my Mother's Closett I found this Jewell which belongs to the family and as I find it has been the former Custome that the Lady Petre should keep it I Deliver it into Your Custody You being the only surviving Lady'. Afterwards, he recalled her reply: 'Brother you may be assured that I shall endeavour to keep it as safe as my owne to that intent, and I hope Brother you will thinke of makeing Choice of some Lady that will make both you and the family happy to whom I may deliver up my trust.' Since he felt that the Dowager was entitled to keep the pearls during her lifetime, Lord Thomas did not ask for them back when he married, expecting that she would leave instructions for their return to him when she died. Instead, in 1695 'the said Lady Dowager by her will deviseth the said Jewell to her daughter Mary, wife of George Heneage'. Mrs Heneage refused to return the pearls, and so Lord Thomas was obliged to take legal action. The importance of the pearls, and the right of the consort and widow to wear them during her lifetime, is reflected in the depositions, some of which have been quoted above. Although it seems certain that the dispute was resolved in favour of Lord Thomas, the pearls are not listed in the Petre family inventory of 1732.

Just as the Petre pearls can no longer be identified, few of those listed in other inventories and worn in seventeenth-century portraits can be traced today. A necklace of large Tay pearls − those found in native mussels − at Drummond Castle is therefore a quite remarkable survival: the pearls were collected over several years by the Puritan Lady Anne Gordon who married the third Earl of Perth in 1639.

Three pear pearls of great historical interest hang from a diamond necklace with two diamond drops bequeathed by Sarah, wife of John first Duke of Marlborough, to her grandson John Spencer which are in the possession of the present Earl Spencer. The pearls were a gift from the City of London to the Princess Royal on her marriage in 1613 to the Elector Palatine and future King of Bohemia and were inherited by her son Prince Rupert: they were sold by Ruperta Hughes, his daughter. The two diamond drops could be the 'paire of diamond pendants' which the Duchess of Marlborough bought at the sale of the jewels of the Duchess of Shrewsbury in 1726, and the forty diamonds of the necklace were a gift from Queen Anne, from her Stuart inheritance.

Queen Anne

The ascendancy of diamond jewellery began with the reign of Queen Anne. Lighting improved and thereafter more entertainments took place in the evening by candlelight: in this atmosphere the flash and sparkle of brilliant and rose-cut diamonds eclipsed all other stones. Although most of the peeresses at Queen Anne's coronation of 1702 wore diamond necklaces, few have survived intact. Some have been sold — anonymously — at Christie's but most suffered the fate of almost all eighteenth-century jewellery and were remounted by the Victorians. Thus the Queen Anne diamond necklace which Lady Middleton wears in her portrait by Winterhalter painted in 1863 was broken up soon after (Plate 140).

The sober yet grand style of late-seventeenth and early eighteenth-century English jewellery is seen at its best in the ruby and diamond parure — that is matching set — owned by the Earls of Rosse until the mid 1970s and now in a private collection. The earrings are girandoles — they branch out like the arms of a candelabra into three drops from a top cluster — and the large brooch is called a stomacher for it occupies much of the space between neckline and waist.

In her correspondence Sarah Duchess of Marlborough said she had adopted from a fashion she had seen in Holland a new way of wearing her husband's miniature set in a slide threaded onto ribbon at the wrist. There is one in the Devonshire collection at Chatsworth, enamelled with the miniature of a man in wig and armour (Plate 57) and with crowned ducal monogram at the back where there are two loops for the ribbon to pass through (Plate 58).

Plate 57. Bracelet miniature of a nobleman in wig and armour, to wear on a ribbon.

Plate 58. The back of the bracelet miniature, showing the crowned ducal monogram, with loops for threading ribbon.

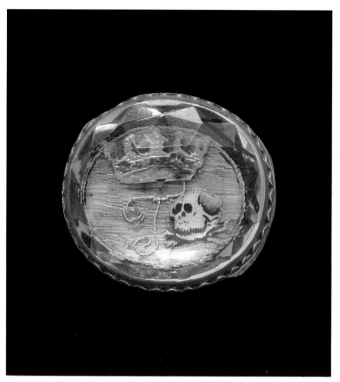

Plate 59. Crystal memorial slide with hair and crowned cipher T commemorating John Marquis of Tullibardine, killed at Malplaquet on 31 August 1709.

Plate 60. Back view of the Tullibardine memorial slide, showing the inscription and loops.

Plate 61. Memento mori locket ring, eye sockets, nostrils and crossbones studded with diamonds.

A similar slide at Blair Castle commemorates the death of the gallant twenty-four-year-old Marquis of Tullibardine who fell at Malplaquet in 1709, and whose hair, crowned initial T and a skull is set under the crystal cover. It served as a pass during the 1715 uprising for the restoration of the House of Stuart, when his younger brother supported the Jacobites (Plates 59 and 60). A more luxurious memorial jewel is in the Rosebery collection: it is a ring with white enamel skull and eye sockets studded with rose-cut diamonds (Plate 61).

Children's Jewels

High-born children were brought up to wear jewels as a sign of rank. Some were practical, such as the 'child's whisell [whistle] set in diamonds' in the 1644 inventory of the Earl of Roxburgh. So too were the coral amulets which helped with teething. The charming gold-mounted coral which belonged to the Duke of Monmouth is displayed at Bowhill House near his portrait as an infant where it is shown hanging round his neck.

Rings were made for little fingers, and were used to celebrate child betrothals. To please their mutual grandmother a marriage was arranged in 1692 between the four-year-old heiress Catherine Apsley, and her eight-year-old cousin Allen Bathurst. Catherine was given a wedding ring and a keeper to ensure it did not fall off. She kept both as a pledge of her engagement to her cousin and twelve years later their union was solemnised in the grandest style which their aunt Lady Wentworth enthusiastically described in a letter to Lord Raby: 'it was a charming sight, he looked very handsom and soe did she look charmingly al in white, he cloath & she sattin & in jewels all the town might have seen they wear soe wel drest & loocked soe beautiful'. They lived at Cirencester Park, home of the Bathursts, where their daughter Lady Leonora Urmstòn's family tree showing their descent and relationship, and the two rings, were preserved with her note asking, 'When I dye I beg these rings and my father's and mother's pictures may be given to the person who shall at that time be Head of the family whoever it may happen to be.'

Plate 62. Gold cross set with rose-cut diamonds on a ribbon threaded through a slide, worn by the first Duchess of Atholl.

Three
THE EARLY GEORGIANS

Jewels were as important to the eighteenth-century British nobility as retainers, carriages and fine houses in broad parklands. They were worn at home in town and country, as well as at the balls, masquerades, regattas and other amusements held at Ranelagh Gardens, and at the theatre where the peeresses sat in the dress circle decked out with plumes and sparkling with diamonds. More than anywhere else they were paraded — and noticed — at court. Family prestige was at stake when the bride of the eldest son and heir made her first appearance before royalty and judgment was passed on her clothes and jewellery. No-one was better qualified to do this than Mrs Delany, a woman of great taste who observed the fashions at the courts of the first three Georges and described them in her letters. Few people impressed Mrs Delany more than Georgiana Poyntz when she called on the Prince and Princess of Wales shortly after her marriage in December 1755 to John Spencer, great-grandson of Sarah Duchess of Marlborough and heir to much of her vast fortune. He rode in his carriage attended by his stepfather Lord Cowper, and three footmen, and was followed by the bride's mother and sister in another carriage accompanied by three more footmen. Then came his bride dressed in white and silver, seated in a sedan chair lined with white satin, escorted by her footmen and preceded by her black page. Both the bride and bridegroom wore the Marlborough diamonds: his shoe-buckles alone

cost £30,000, and Mrs Delany was fascinated by her earrings three drops all diamonds, no paltry scrolls of silver. Her necklace most perfect brilliants, the middle stone worth £1,000, set at the edge with small brilliants — the large diamonds meet in this manner. Her cap all brilliants made in the fashion of a small butterfly skeleton had a very good effect of a pompom, and behind, where you may suppose the bottom of the caul, a knot of diamonds and two little puffs of diamonds where the lappets are fastened and two shaking sprigs for her hair: six roses all brilliants for her stays...Her watch and etuy suited to the rest and a seal of Mercury cut in a very fine turquoise stone set as a standing for a spaniel dog, the body of the pearl the size of the Duchess of Portland's dolphin, the head and neck made out of gold finely wrought, two little brilliants for its eyes and a brilliant collar: it cost 70 guineas. All these things I have just seen at Mrs Spencer's who looked at them with the utmost unconcern though not insensible to their merit as fine of their kind but as the least part of her happiness.

The Nabobs

Competing with the splendour of those like the Spencers who were born to high rank and large fortunes were the nabobs, described by Lord Macaulay as people 'of neither opulent or ancient families sent to the East at an early age and who returned with large fortunes which they exhibited insolently and spent extravagantly'. They transferred some of their

Plate 63. Lady Elizabeth Keppel — later Marchioness of Tavistock — in the dress and jewellery she wore as bridesmaid to Queen Charlotte, painted by Sir Joshua Reynolds in 1761.

Plate 64. Nabob family emerald and pearl necklace with Mughal
carved emerald pendant, *c*. 1720.

money home as gemstones and pearls which were
ultimately destined to replenish old family jewel caskets when their children married into the aristocracy
(Plate 64).

The most distinguished of all nabobs, Robert Clive,
first Lord Clive, (1725-75) lived as splendidly as a
blue-blooded grandee on an income of at least £61,000
a year. In 1767 he ordered new parures for his wife
from the leading London jeweller, Peter Duval, set
with stones from the collection he had acquired in
India. These stones were part of the inheritance
of his children and grandchildren, one of whom,
Charlotte Florentia, married the third Duke of
Northumberland in 1817. The Londonderry family
benefited from a nabob connection too. The Down
diamonds, which are still in the family collection,
were part of the fortune amassed by Sir Robert Cowan
while Governor of Bombay (see Appendix). He left
them to his sister Mary who married Alexander
Stewart of County Down in 1736; they were the
parents of the first Marquess.

Fashion and Design

Ever since the Middle Ages the Paris jewellers had
led the rest of Europe. As part of his duties Queen
Elizabeth's ambassador there, Sir Nicholas Throck-
morton, had kept a look out for new and beautiful
designs, and in the seventeenth century Parisian
jewellers reached a peak of excellence thanks to the
patronage of the extravagant and luxury-loving court
of Louis XIV. Many were Protestants, and after their
religious freedom was withdrawn by the Revocation
of the Edict of Nantes in 1685 Huguenot goldsmiths
and jewellers emigrated to Britain, bringing with them
the skills which enabled the London trade to compete
with Paris for the first time in its history. The success of the leading Huguenots — Elias Russell, Peter
Dutens, Peter and John Duval — in obtaining aristocratic patronage made life difficult for some of the
English jewellers. When Andrew Hunter offered the
Duke of Bedford a diamond nosegay for his daughter,
Lady Caroline, to wear with her bridesmaid's dress

at the wedding of King George III and Queen Charlotte in 1761, he complained, 'I have met lately with some things that have not gone quite to my mind having been supplanted by foreigners'. His experience is borne out by archival evidence, for the majority of the accounts for jewels bought by the nobility are from Huguenots, and are often written in French. These bills are important, for they are often all that remains of the Huguenot jewellery which vanished long ago.

Sir Joshua Reynolds's portrait of Lady Elizabeth Keppel, who was to marry the Marquis of Tavistock in 1764, dressed as a bridesmaid for the royal wedding, illustrates how jewellery was worn at a great court occasion in the early years of the reign of King George III. She is ravishing in silver and white with diamonds flashing out from her hair, ears and neck.

A tall spray of leaves and flowers to the side, and the clusters pinned above the brow emphasise her small neat powdered head (Plate 63). The jewelled birds — doves, eagles, pigeons — peacock feathers, butterflies, moths and crescent moons also worn in the hair at the time were fitted with trembler springs to give extra glitter and sparkle.

From the 1760s tiaras inspired by antiquity came into fashion (Plate 65): according to family tradition the elegant tiara which Lady Diana Spencer wore over her wedding veil when she married the Prince of Wales in 1981 was made for her ancestress, the Viscountess Montagu, in 1767. Although the design of open scrolls enclosing star-shaped flowers and leaves cannot be attributed to a particular maker it is in that fine Huguenot style which influenced early Georgian jewellery.

Plate 65. Sir Osbert Sitwell's diamonds shown at the Exhibition of the Four Georges in London in 1931.

Earrings

In spite of the ordeal of piercing which had to be endured, earrings were essential to the appearance of the well-dressed woman, for whether dressed high or low the hair was always drawn back showing the ears. When Lady Tavistock sat for her portrait she wore a version of the seventeenth-century girandole (Plate 66) with the tops linked to the three pendent drops by ribbon bows interspersed with floral sprays. Those who could afford them preferred diamonds, which lit up the face. Augusta Duchess of Brunswick gave a pair made of diamonds with pearls to her god-daughter Augusta, who married Sir James Cockburn, in top and drop style, 'set with small brilliants with pearl drop centres and pendants'. These were eventually sold by Christie's on 9 June 1902. The elaborate 'old English emerald and diamond ear-pendants each composed of a pear-shaped emerald drop with semi-circles of five diamonds at the base and supported by three stone diamond chains to a single pear-shaped diamond drop' sold by Christie's on 15 November 1950 were designed to be worn with the very high coiffures fashionable in the 1780s.

Plate 66. Diamond girandole earrings. Lady Elizabeth Keppel wears a similar pair in her portrait (see Plate 63).

Necklaces

The velvet choker worn round Lady Tavistock's neck in her portrait is embellished with a band of jewels; hanging down in front is an 'esclavage' or jewelled chain of flowers entwined with ribbons. Sadly, no English example of this graceful rococo design seems to have survived. Less rare are the necklaces of stones set in plain clusters or 'rivières' of single collets, which according to the correspondence of Lady Louisa Connolly, chatelaine of the superb Castletown in Ireland, were the height of fashion in 1776 (Plate 65). Sometimes the lines of graduated stones were spaced by small diamond points, and girandole or single drops framed in ribbons hung from the centre. Pendent crosses hung either high on the neck from jewelled or ribbon chokers or low from the esclavage. Whether of Greek or Latin form the cross looked best when set with fine quality rose- or brilliant-cut diamonds. Miniatures of loved ones framed in jewelled borders were also worn hanging from the neck as well as in rings and at the wrist.

Brooches

One of the most beautiful pieces of eighteenth-century jewellery was bought by the notorious Duke of Wharton (1698-1731), lampooned as

a wild Peer
So known for his rakish tricks

for Maria Theresa, maid of honour to the Queen of Spain, whom he married as his second wife in 1726. It is a tuft of five peacock's feathers, exquisitely set with aquamarines and rose diamonds, and is in the collection at Southside House (Plate 67). Two others illustrate the mid-century fashion for large brooches: one is a diamond bouquet of cornflowers, their stems tied with a ribbon (Plate 68), eventually sold by Christie's on 2 June 1955; the other is an impressive bowknot with ribbons meeting at a cluster and pendants hanging from it (Plate 69). This stomacher is

Plate 67. Acquamarine and rose diamond peacock-feather aigrette, worn by the Duchess of Wharton, c. 1726.

Plate 68 (*left*). George III cornflower and wild flower brooch, the stems tied with a ribbon bow, all set with diamonds.

Plate 69 (*above*). Diamond stomacher bowknot, the double ribbon loops meeting at a cluster. This brooch is remarkable for its size.

now owned by a noble north country family. More severe in design is the diamond brooch of symmetrical scrollwork surrounding a yellow diamond centre, with pendants, which has the monogram of the naturalist and explorer Sir Joseph Banks (1740-1820) at the back: it was a present to his wife, 'the comely and modest' Dorothea Hugesson whom he married in 1779, and is now privately owned (Plate 70).

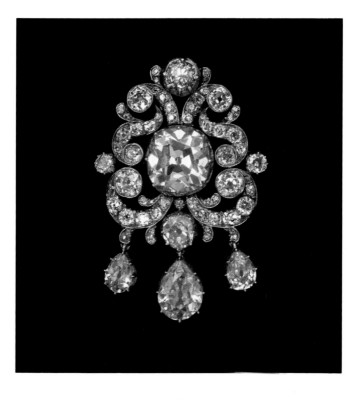

Plate 70 (*left*). Diamond scrollwork brooch centred on a yellow diamond. Given by Sir Joseph Banks to his wife Dorothea at the time of their marriage in 1779.

Plate 71 (*opposite*). The Marchioness of Rockingham's mother-of-pearl bracelets with carnival mask clasps.

Bracelets

Rows of pearls were fastened with jewelled or enamelled clasps reflecting personal taste and sentiment. The pair enamelled with women's faces, cheeks and chins dotted flirtatiously with patches, their rose diamond eyes sparkling through black velvet masks, which belonged to the Marchioness of Rockingham, wife of the Prime Minister, evoke all the gaiety of the masquerade (Plate 71). Others, in the collection of the Earl of Rosebery, set with oval miniatures of nymphs in classical dress dancing to castanets and tambourine, were the choice of a music lover. These are unusual, for most women preferred miniatures of loved ones — mother and father, husband and child, brother and sister — painted on ivory or vellum or else enamelled on gold (Plate 72). In the 1780s silhouettes outlining profiles, like shadows on a white ground, came into fashion: the fourth Duke of Atholl and his Duchess Jane were portrayed by John Miers shortly before her death in 1790. Set in neo-classical bright-cut pointed oval mounts, they are still preserved at Blair Castle (Plate 73).

Plate 72. Bracelet clasps with miniatures of John Spencer and his sister Diana, children of the Hon. John Spencer, and worn by their mother.

Plate 73. Bracelet clasps with silhouettes of the fourth Duke of Atholl and his wife Jane, by John Miers.

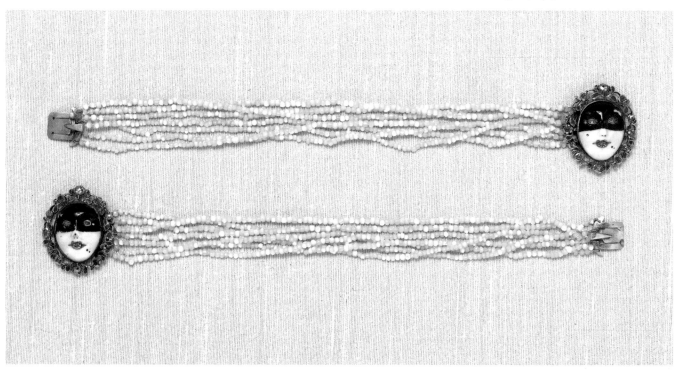

Rings

Giardinetti – little gardens – decorative rings set with small coloured stones and rose diamonds in sprays of flowers, leaves and fruit were given as presents and a woman of means might own several. One of the few provenanced giardinetti rings is the pomegranate worn by Charlotte, daughter and heiress of the second Duke of Atholl, who married her cousin John, the future third Duke, in 1753. The Duke and Duchess commissioned fine furniture and a family group portrait from Johann Zoffany which he painted in 1765-7. The ring shows their excellent taste in jewellery (Plate 74). It was sold by Christie's on 5 October 1988.

Rings set with more valuable and larger stones had a slim chance of survival unless they belonged to some distinguished person whose memory was particularly respected. Thus the Duchess of Argyll bequeathed her 'diamond ring set with one large brilliant' in 1767 to her son-in-law John Earl of Bute, with a note explaining that her husband the great soldier, the second Duke of Argyll, had worn it during all his campaigns in the reign of Queen Anne. The present whereabouts is not known.

The inside of a plain hoop ring at Grimsthorpe Castle inscribed THO FARE APERT YET NEIR IN HEART is one of the large category of love rings with mottoes or posies – little poems – in English. They were also used as wedding rings and the posy was composed for the occasion with the help of literary friends. The same sentiments are expressed by love mottoes in French for it was not uncommon for the aristocracy to correspond in that language. A flirtatious letter at Chatsworth written by Georgiana Duchess of Devonshire to the Prince of Wales on 11 December 1786, thanking him for his present of a jewelled key – 'the prettiest ornament I ever saw' – begins, 'Mon cher, cher frère' and continues, 'je garderai bien les secrets de votre coeur' (I will keep safe the secrets of your heart). Illustrating the same fashion are three rings at Woburn Abbey with the hoops enamelled on the outside with the mottoes: UNIS PAR UN DOUX LIEN, DONNE PAR L'AMITIE, and L [meaning Elle—She] ME RAPELLE UNE AMIE. (United by a tender bond. Given in friendship. She (the ring) is a memento of my love). Their message is often emphasised by the presence of a heart – single, twinned, winged or burning – on the bezel or concealed within. There is

Plate 74. Pomegranate ring worn by Charlotte, wife of the third Duke of Atholl.

a locket ring of this type in the Rosebery collection (Plate 75): the carnival mask bezel contains a heart with the declaration POUR VOUS SEULE (For you alone) (Plate 76). Love mottoes are also linked with the theme of time. A ring from a Scottish collection with clock dial bezel was inscribed J'AIME A TOUT HEURE (sold at Christie's on 24 June 1946) and, equally aptly, another which was in the Spencer collection (sold by S.J. Phillips in 1978) LE TEMPS NOUS JOINDRA (Time will unite us).

The solicitous inscription VOUS AURE SOIN DE VOTRE SANTE SI VOUS SOUHAITE MON REPOS (You will keep well if you wish me peace of mind) is enamelled on the outside of the hoop of a rather more important ring set with an onyx cameo of the infant Hercules. This too came from the Spencer collection (sold by S.J. Phillips in 1978). The first Earl Spencer and his Countess Georgiana were very proud of another ring set with a moss agate cameo of a leopard. This remarkably realistic study was a gift from the connoisseur Cardinal Albani to the great soldier, Prince Eugène of Savoy, who left it to his niece. It was subsequently in the collection of Antonio Maria Zanetti, a man of great taste who refused all offers — even from Horace Walpole — until the Spencers, while in Venice buying works of art, persuaded him to part with it. On their way home they met the actor-manager David Garrick, who was also in Italy, and he describes the ring in a letter to the Duke of Devonshire in the Chatsworth archives. It was sold by S.J. Phillips in 1978.

This was the great age of cameo collecting and some people liked to wear their favourite stones in jewels, particularly rings. The second Duke of Devonshire — whose great collection is still at Chatsworth — set an acquamarine intaglio of the Roman Empress Sabina in a signet for his own personal use with his monogram and ducal coronet on the back. From Lorenz Natter, a German engraver, the Marquess of Rockingham commissioned a cornelian intaglio portrait of his wife Mary whom he married in 1752, and which he wore in a plain Roman-style gold ring. This was sold by Christie's on 19 March 1980.

Memorial rings commemorated the loss of friends and family. The stock designs can be seen in the

Plate 75 (*top*). Locket ring with carnival mask framed in rubies, a Rosebery heirloom.

Plate 76 (*above*). The inside of the Rosebery carnival ring, showing French inscription and heart.

Plate 77. Mourning rings commemorating friends and relations, collected throughout the eighteenth century and preserved at Grimsthorpe Castle.

collection of eighteenth-century rings spanning eight decades still preserved at Grimsthorpe Castle. They are inscribed with the names of members of the family and some famous contemporaries, among them the first Earl of Hardwicke, Lord Chief Justice from 1737 to 1756, and Thomas Secker (1693–1768), Archbishop of Canterbury (Plate 77). The tragic loss of the male heir to a noble house is recalled by the memorial ring to Edward, infant son of the second Earl of Oxford, who lived for only five days. The octagonal bezel is set with a superb emerald: symbols of burning lamps are at each corner and hair is enclosed in two panels at the sides. At the back a shield is brightly enamelled with the arms: Harley quartering Vere Bampton and Cavendish and the motto FIDE ET VIRTUTE (Faith and virtue). The inside of the hoop — enamelled white for an unmarried person — is inscribed UNE VIE SI COURTE UNE SI GRANDE AFFLICTION (Such a short life, such a great sorrow) and the outside EDWARD HARLEY NAT 18 OCT 1725 OB 22 OCT 1725. This was sold by Sotheby's on 25 November 1976. The quality is so remarkable that it could be easily assumed that the emerald ring is unique but it seems that there were two, for the catalogue of objects of vertu at Welbeck Abbey lists another, this time set with a sapphire. It was as a consequence of the death of the infant Lord Harley that his sister Margaret brought to her marriage to the second Duke of Portland in 1734 the estate of Welbeck in Nottingham as well as the London properties around Oxford Street and Portland Place.

Memorial Lockets

Another touching memorial jewel is the locket at Blair Castle worn by the fourth Duchess of Atholl which contained curls of her own hair, of the Duke and each of their seven children, all pinned to tiny pearl crowns and labelled. It testifies to the domestic happiness evident from a group portrait of the family enjoying the Highland landscape nearby. By David Allan, it can be seen at Blair Castle. The Duchess was also devoted to her brother Charles, a Colonel in the army who died at the age of twenty-nine. The locket she wore in his memory contains his hair woven into a basket pattern under glass, and framed like a picture in a border inscribed IN MEMORY OF OUR DEAREST BROTHER CHARLES OH LOSS IRREPARABLE, and at the back THE HON CHARLES CATHCART DIED JUNE IOTH 1788 ON HIS EMBASSY TO CHINA ON BOARD THE VESTAL FRIGATE ON THE HEIGHTS OF BANCA, with verses composed by the Duchess:

tho' raised above
The reach of human pain above the flight
Of human joy yet with a mingled ray
Of sadly pleas'd remembrance must thou feel
A sister's tender love a sister's tender woe.

J.A. (Jane Atholl)

Locks of hair were treasured as tokens of deep friendship. Mrs Delany was overjoyed when Queen Charlotte gave her a pearl locket ornamented with the royal crown and cipher with 'a lock of her beautiful hair: so precious a gift is indeed inestimable'. The eccentric traveller and obsessive royalist, Lady Mary Coke, was not so fortunate. Having been warmly received by the Empress Maria Theresa in Vienna in 1772, she was most put out when the imperial gift of a bracelet clasp finally arrived but without the precious hair inside, as she had been expecting: 'the cipher of the Empress in diamonds set round with diamonds close and another border of diamonds round that... 'tis extremely pretty set & the value to me very great coming from her. 'Tis some small disappointment that Her Majestie's hair is not under the cipher as I had some reason to flatter myself I should have had that favour which would have been more to me than all the diamonds in the world.' Lady Mary left her pearl bracelet with the clasp (Plate 78) to her favourite niece Elizabeth, whom she described as 'like a little angel, her behaviour the prettiest in the world, cheerful, good-humoured and proper in all respects. I believe her as sensible as she is handsome'. Elizabeth married the third Duke of Buccleuch and Queensberry in 1767 and the pearl bracelet and clasp has been worn by the Duchesses of Buccleuch and Queensberry ever since (Plate 79).

Royal Gifts

During their long reign King George III and Queen Charlotte made many gifts, principally of miniatures and watches. The Duchess of Ancaster, Mistress of the Robes 1761-93, wore the Queen's gift of her miniature at the waist hanging from a broad sash, like an order. As the Duchess of Hamilton was always late for her duties as Lady of the Bedchamber (1761-84), and blamed her watch, the Queen gave her a new one, making a joke about it. These gifts

Plate 78 (*top*). Bracelet clasp with diamond cipher of the Empress Maria Theresa of Austria, given by her to Lady Mary Coke in 1772.

Plate 79 (*above*). The Duchess of Buccleuch in 1897 dressed as Elizabeth Duchess of Buccleuch: the Maria Theresa bracelet clasp is on her wrist.

Plate 80 (*top*). Devonshire family chatelaine. The oval medallions enclose hair identified by the cipher GHC and by the Cavendish snakes.

Plate 81 (*above*). Lady Evelyn Cavendish as a lady at the court of the Empress of Austria in 1897 with the Devonshire chatelaine at her waist.

have vanished, but the suite of chatelaine, watch and miniature which were given to the Viscount and Viscountess Harcourt are still owned by the family (plate 82). As Master of the Horse the Viscount Harcourt escorted the future Queen Charlotte from her home in Mecklenburg Strelitz in 1761 and two years later he was appointed Lord Chamberlain. All these pieces are enamelled deep blue twinkling with tiny rose-diamond stars, and the royal cipher GR is on the watch and the miniature of the King. The watch with movement by Justin Vulliamy is dated 1750. Dorothea, wife of Sir Joseph Banks, who received gifts of jewellery from the Queen, left them to her nephew Sir Edward Knatchbull. A garnet suite was sold one hundred years later, at Christie's on 8 June 1893, followed by a chrysolite parure and set of rose diamond buttons sold in aid of the Red Cross by Christie's on 26 March 1917.

Queen Marie Antoinette

The name of Queen Marie Antoinette is associated with the famous necklace set with 647 stones made by Böhmer and Bassange, and offered to Louis XVI to give the Queen on the birth of their first child in 1778. The Queen refused it, and shortly after the necklace was stolen by a syndicate led by a Madame de la Motte, and broken up. Stones from the esclavage were brought to London by Monsieur de la Motte who sold twenty-two of them to Robert Gray of Bond Street, explaining that they had been removed from a stomacher he had inherited from his mother. They were mounted in a rivière bought by the first Duke of Sutherland for his wife Elizabeth, Countess of Sutherland in her own right. The discriminating Mrs Delany admired her greatly: 'a wonderful woman having preserved such simplicity of manners amid the great attention that has been paid her'. The necklace is a Sutherland heirloom (Plate 85) and always causes a sensation when worn (Plate 86). Early in the reign of Edward VII Viscount Esher remembered Duchess Millicent at a ball at Stafford House, 'at the top of the stairs all in black with the gorgeous Marie Antoinette necklace round her throat was a sight not easily forgotten'. Other stones were bought by the jeweller Nathaniel Jeffreys of Piccadilly and

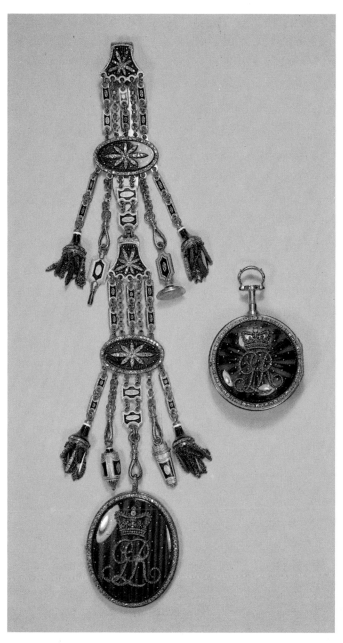

Plate 82. Chatelaine with miniature and watch bearing the royal ciphers, presented by King George III and Queen Charlotte to Viscount and Viscountess Harcourt.

Plate 83. Chatelaine with miniatures of a Muse and a lady.

Plate 84. The seal of the chatelaine illustrated above, engraved with the Pelham buckle, badge of the Earl of Yarborough, who is the present owner.

made into a necklace for Miss Arabella Cope by the third Duke of Dorset at the time of their marriage in 1790: he had announced that he wanted to cover her in diamonds. The necklace was broken up to make a tiara by Lady Sackville around 1900 (Plate 264).

Whereas these superb diamonds were never in Queen Marie Antoinette's possession, being far too opulent for her, the buckle she gave as a keepsake to Georgiana Duchess of Devonshire reflected her own taste. The Duchess wore it in 1784 to a ball given by the French ambassador, Count d'Adhémar: 'I had a white gauze pettycoat, an apron bound with black, my sash with the Queen of France's pearl buckle under my gown and a Robe turke of white gauze clouded with black and a kind of Spanish gauze hat with feathers hanging down, a gauze puffing handkerchief bound with black and a great nosegay of cornflowers.' In 1801 she gave it to her own daughter Georgiana, set in the centre of a pearl necklace, as a present for her marriage with the future Earl of Carlisle. It was returned to Chatsworth in 1858.

Queen Marie Antoinette's affection for Duchess Georgiana was resented by English visitors to France who came away with the impression that the Queen considered her the most important person in England. However, theirs was a friendship of long standing dating back to 1774, the year when Marie Antoinette became Queen of France, for Duchess Georgiana's mother, Countess Spencer (the former Georgiana Poyntz) had the entrée to the French court. Outraged by the execution of the French king and queen, the Countess may have commissioned in their memory a black enamel ring with twin bands inscribed MARIE ANTOINETTE LOUIS XVI IMMOLES EN FRANCE PLEURES EN ANGLETERRE (Marie Antoinette Louis XVI Murdered in France Mourned in England) and the dates 21 JAN 16 OCT 1793 inside. It was kept at Althorp until sold by S.J. Phillips in 1978.

In 1960 Earl Spencer lent a diadem said to have belonged to Queen Marie Antoinette to the exhibition

Plate 85 (*top*). The Sutherland necklace. The diamonds are from the famous Marie Antoinette necklace.

Plate 86 (*left*). Duchess 'Blair', second wife of the third Duke, wearing the Sutherland necklace.

of jewellery held in Birmingham. Given by the banker Lord Revelstoke to his daughter Margaret Baring when she married the sixth Earl Spencer in 1887, it was described in the exhibition catalogue as 'rose cut diamonds composed of graduated flower sprays in pear shaped diamond frames resting on diamond scrolls terminating in trefoils on a base of two rows of diamonds with a band of blue enamel on gold'. Elegant jewels of this type associated with romantic historical figures are rare: one of the few, the pink diamond ring once owned by Madame du Barry who succeeded Madame de Pompadour as mistress of Louis XV, is now in the collection of the Duke of Northumberland. It was acquired by the third Duke when he represented King George IV at the coronation of Charles X in Paris in 1825.

The Jacobites

A group of eighteenth-century British jewellery survives as evidence of Jacobite loyalty to the Stuarts, exiled by the Revolution of 1688. Although the intrinsic value is nearly always small their historical interest is great, for these 'treasonable jewels' were worn by those brave enough to face imprisonment and death for their devotion to the cause. Although Jacobite hopes had been crushed by the failure of the 1715 uprising and the Hanoverian accession, they were rekindled again in 1745 by the arrival of Prince Charles Edward who, in spite of having neither money nor arms, succeeded through sheer charisma in raising an army and leading it within reach of London. Those who helped him in this great adventure were given tokens to remember him by. In Lancashire he stayed with a high-Tory squire, Mr Winckley of Brockholes, whose granddaughter Lady Shelley recalled: 'We were all strong Jacobites — in our old house the Pretender had slept the night before the Battle of Preston and I still possess the bracelet given by him to my ancestor with a portrait of King Charles made of his own hair cut off the scaffold and dipped in his blood. I recall the pride with which I wore this bracelet on state occasions.'

Plate 87 (*top*). Jacobite ring given by Prince Charles Edward to Thomas Cholmondeley in 1745.

Plate 88 (*right*). A view of the royal crown on the shoulder of the Jacobite ring, with a cuirass beneath.

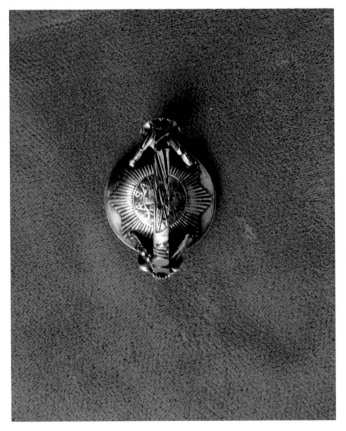

In contrast with this pathetic relic of the execution of King Charles I, the ring which Prince Charles Edward gave a Cheshire gentleman, Thomas Cholmondeley, summons up all the pageantry of war with its panoply of arms — helmet, drum, the flag of St Andrew, trumpets, breast-plate and sword — round the hoop (Plate 89). The Stuart emblems of the white rose of York and the royal crown flank the bezel which is set with a magnificent moss agate representing the thistle of Scotland (Plate 87). At the back the inscription CAESAR CAESARIS frames the green star of the Order of the Thistle. This remarkable ring is still owned by a descendant.

The Prince's leading Welsh supporter was Sir Watkin Williams Wynn: he gave him a ruby ring framed in a crowned and buckled Garter inscribed with the royal motto DIEU ET MON DROIT on the hoop. Some years later Flora Macdonald, who helped the Prince escape capture after his defeat by the army of the Duke of Cumberland, gave Lady Watkin Williams Wynn a pair of onyx earrings, as a keepsake. They were lent to the jewellery exhibition held at the Victoria and Albert Museum in 1872 with Lady Watkin Williams Wynn's round gold badge enamelled with the white rose of York. She wore this hanging from a diamond bow as patroness of the Cycle of the White Rose, a club founded in 1710 by the Jacobite gentry of Wales and Cheshire. Meetings were held at the houses of the different members in turn and toasts drunk to the king across the water.

The majority of Jacobite jewels are in Scotland, where Stuart supporters were both numerous and active. Lady Strathallan, imprisoned in Edinburgh Castle in 1746, wore the Prince's miniature enamelled by C.F. Zincke hanging from a diamond and ruby cluster necklace. This was sold by Christie's on 9 July 1935. Another miniature of the Prince was painted while he breakfasted at Blair Castle at the beginning of the campaign of 1745: a mid-nineteenth-century Duchess of Atholl wore it in a bracelet, which is still there. Also at Blair Castle is a ring inscribed JAMES THE 8TH KING OF SCOTLAND CHEVALIER

Plate 89 (*top*). A view of the shoulder of the Cholmondeley Jacobite ring, showing the white rose of York.

Plate 90 (*left*). The back of the Cholmondeley ring, enamelled with star of the Order of the Thistle and motto.

DE ST GEORGE, the name of the Old Pretender, and a rock crystal locket which contains a lock of Prince Charles Edward's hair and a piece of his tartan.

Not everyone dared display their loyalty openly. The owner of the fine early-eighteenth-century memorial ring to King Charles I with miniature framed in Garter blue and hoop inscribed PRO PATRIA NON TIMIDUS MORI (Do not fear death for your country) wore it concealed within a broad keeper hoop: both ring and keeper are in the collection of the Duke of Hamilton at Lennoxlove (Plate 91).

The Stuart relics of the Duke of Buccleuch and Queensberry at Drumlanrig Castle make a strong appeal to the imagination. Rings set with cameos represent the people involved: the Old Pretender, his wife Clementina Sobieska, their sons and their daughter-in-law Princess Louisa of Stolberg. Each ring is a monument of Jacobite history and none more so than 'Prince Charles Edward's wedding ring'. The bezel is set with a turquoise cameo crown

framed in brilliants: concealed inside is a miniature of the Prince. The inscription on the hoop BY EVERY CLAIM TIS YOURS refers to the crown. Engraved round the back and sides of the bezel are emblems of majesty — laurel wreath, sceptre with dove, and hand of justice — and the inscription UD R DD AD NUPTIAS 1772, the date of his marriage with Princess Louisa of Stolberg. A smaller ring, also set with a turquoise cameo crown, is inscribed within and without the hoop THOU SHALT TO FORTUNE VIRTUE RECONCILE BOTH DUE TO HIM, and with initials — whose significance is not known — round the sides of the bezel. There are the emblems of pink and white thistles on the shoulders and a small pink heart at the base of the hoop. The collection, which was acquired by Lady John Scott in the early nineteenth century, reflects the enthusiasm for the cause revived by Sir Walter Scott's Jacobite saga, *Redgauntlet* (1824), long after it had ceased to be a political threat.

Plate 91. Jacobite Garter ring with miniature of King Charles I, the hoop inscribed PRO PATRIA NON TIMUDUS MORI. It was worn concealed beneath the gold keeper ring.

Four
THE LATER GEORGIANS

Napoleon's war against England was good for business – at least for Rundell, Bridge and Rundell, the court jewellers on Ludgate Hill. George Fox, a retired salesman, traced their huge success back to 1803, when, 'on war breaking out again with France, and the consequent advance of Rents generally, the Nobility and Gentry seemed anxious to vie with each other in every species of Luxury and extravagance and such orders were given for splendid services and costly suits of jewels as had not been before thought of.' The firm had a reputation for quality and the basis of their fortune was a stock of pearls and gemstones bought by the shrewd Mr Rundell from unfortunate French émigrés at the time of the Revolution. His partner, Mr Bridge, was the ace salesman who set out on his rounds from the shop every morning with a blue bag well fitted out with jewels, calling first at Buckingham Palace and Carlton House and then at the houses of all the nobility and gentry, 'beating the buck out of doors to drive the game to Ludgate Hill'. His strategy worked well: in the afternoon from three till seven at night Ludgate Hill was crowded with the carriages of dukes and duchesses, marquesses and marchionesses, earls and countesses securing the handsome services of plate and the superb jewels which passed down to their Victorian and Edwardian heirs and successors.

The lead came from George Prince of Wales, whose sense of the superb and magnificent attracted him to

jewellery no less than to art and architecture. His family acknowledged his excellent taste as a young man by delegating their jewellery purchases to him, and he bought prodigally for himself and the various women in his life. 'Fairyland', is how the American ambassador, Richard Rush, described the jewelled scene at one of the Prince's receptions at Carlton House. As for the Queen's Drawing Room in 1818:

No lady was without her plume. The whole was a waving field of feathers. Some were blue like the sky, tinged with red, here you saw violet and yellow, there shades of green. But most were like tufts of snow. The diamonds encircling them caught the sun through the windows and threw dazzling beams around...each lady seemed to rise out of a gilded little barricade or one of silvery texture. Thus topped by her plume, and the face divine interposing gave to the whole an effect so unique, so fraught with feminine grace and grandeur that it seemed as if a curtain had risen to show a pageant in another sphere.

London society was now more splendid than ever: the bon ton flocked to Almack's and the opera, there were at least twenty balls each night of the season as well as dinners, masquerades and water-parties. Princely hospitality was dispensed at the great houses of Belvoir, Chatsworth, Longleat and Eaton Hall, where dress was as formal as in London. When the Comtesse de Boigne dined quietly with the Earl and Countess of Liverpool at their country home in 1816,

Plate 92. The Marchioness of Londonderry, painted by A. Dubois-Drahonnet in the dress and jewels she wore to the coronation of King William IV.

Plate 93. Diamond parure set with the famous 'Gouttes de perles'
bought during the Londonderry embassy to Vienna.

Plate 94. A tiara from the 'Gouttes de perles' suite.

Plate 95. Necklace, earrings and brooches set with the Palffy turquoises
bought by the Marchioness of Londonderry in Vienna *c.* 1822.

her hostess wore a gold diadem enriched with precious stones over a veil; the other guest, Lady Mulgrave, was resplendent in satin with jewels and flowers in her hair.

The Marchioness of Londonderry

One of society's greatest amusements was the impersonation of historical characters at costume balls. Frances Anne Vane-Tempest-Stewart, wife of the third Marquess of Londonderry, had the jewels, the style and the audacity to turn such an opportunity into a personal triumph. It was at a costume ball at the Hanover Square Rooms in 1835 that the young Benjamin Disraeli first met her, 'dressed as Cleopatra in a dress literally embroidered with emeralds and diamonds from top to toe. It looked like armour and she like a rhinocerous.'

A great heiress in her own right, Frances Anne inherited the Antrim rubies and emeralds from her mother, the Countess of Antrim, and with the fortune left by her father, Sir Harry Vane-Tempest, she

could afford to buy whatever she wished. On the birth of her eldest son in Vienna in 1821 where her husband was ambassador, she acquired — for £10,000 — the famous Gouttes de Perles, or tear drops, from the widow of a banker, Countess de Fries, and had them made into a regal set of necklace, diadem, comb and earrings (Plates 93 and 94). She also bought a matchless set of large turquoises — her birthstone — from Count Ferdinand Palffy who had spent a lifetime collecting them and believed them to be unique (Plate 95). While in Vienna she was introduced to the Emperor Alexander of Russia. He told her that in 1818 he had seen her portrait in the studio of Sir Thomas Lawrence and had 'felt a sort of foreboding that the person whose picture was before him was fated to have an influence over his destiny and cause him much disquiet'. His intuition proved correct. Having lived like a hermit for the previous ten years he was seized with a romantic passion and continually sought her company. Immensely flattered by the Emperor's attentions, she nonetheless did not lose her head: 'Indeed when memory recalls this too

Plate 96. Diamond and Siberian amethyst chain. The stones were a gift to
the Marchioness of Londonderry from the Emperor Alexander I of Russia.

highly gifted and all perfect being at my feet kneeling before me and covering my hands as he was wont with kisses so far from wondering at my weakness I can only rejoice and wonder that we came out of the ordeal free of guilt.' He gave her gemstones from his vast empire to remember him by: an intense pink topaz, a yellow diamond, and the large Siberian amethysts which clasp the sleeves of the red velvet dress she wears in a portrait by Sir Thomas Lawrence with her small son Viscount Seaham. Later she had the amethysts — of which she was extremely proud — set in a diamond chain which she sometimes wore as a tiara on her head, but more usually across her dress like the ribbon of an order (Plate 96).

After the death of her sister-in-law Emily — widow of the eminent statesman, the second Marquess — in 1829, Frances Anne could wear the Down diamonds from India, brought into the family by Mary Cowan, mother of the first Marquess. With this inheritance came all the diamonds which Viscount Castlereagh (later the second Marquess), then Foreign Secretary, had received from the allied monarchs. Some were

mounted in his Garter insignia and ceremonial sword but others were worn by his wife, as is clear from a letter he wrote from the Foreign Office enclosing a miniature of the King of Naples and Sicily:

Dearest Em,
I send you an ugly face and some pretty diamonds which will become you rather better than his Sicilian Majestys.

Marchioness Frances was painted by A. Dubois-Drahonnet dressed for the coronation of King William IV in 1831 (Plate 92), and many of the jewels she wore then, particularly the belt of Down diamonds, were seen at the Queen's Drawing Room when the *Lady's Magazine* described her

most beautiful white blond lace dress, of the most costly description, and richest manufacture, over a white satin slip; a zone [belt] entirely composed of brilliants. Head-dress, a beautiful and brilliant garland of diamonds with a comb ornamented with large pearls; an esclavage necklace composed of immense pear-shaped pearls and diamonds which is said to be unrivalled in Europe for its beauty and value. Her ladyship also wore a bouquet of costly brilliants at her left breast and three rows of pearls suspended from the left epaulette by a lozenge of brilliants terminating on the right side towards the waist. Headdress: an immense tiara of diamonds surmounted by moveable pieces with a plume of fifteen rich ostrich feathers. The most conspicuous part of this attire was the zone or cincture of brilliants, full two inches in width and consisting of one entire mass of brilliants and divided by the invisible setting of each.

All her life she outshone everybody: after the coronation of Queen Victoria in 1838 Benjamin Disraeli reported to his sister, 'Fanny blazed among the peeresses and looked like an Empress'.

Marchioness Frances took her jewels on her travels. Staying in St Petersburg in 1837 she had the pleasure of showing them to the Empress while one of the grandduchesses made sketches of the pieces her mother liked best. The Empress's favourite was the enamelled gold cross entwined with flowers and set with cabochon rubies and emeralds which had been a wedding present from the Prince Regent (Plate 97). It is an early example of the Gothic revival in English jewellery for not only are the gemstones unfaceted but the back is enamelled with tracery (Plate 98). It may well have come from Rundell, Bridge and Rundell for in 1819 — the date of the marriage with the future third Marquess — they invoiced the Prince for 'a fine antique cross composed of oriental stones, enamel etc.' As a souvenir of this enjoyable afternoon with the imperial family the Empress presented a miniature of herself in national costume, framed in diamonds and mounted in a turquoise bracelet.

George IV

Mrs Fitzherbert, his morganatic wife, who was installed by the Prince in fine houses in London and Brighton, was bedecked by him with jewels. She left them to her adopted daughter Minnie Seymour, wife of Colonel George Dawson-Damer, and they passed to their children, the fourth Earl of Portarlington and the Countess of Fortescue. They consist of a ring with a miniature of the Prince's eye by Richard Cosway, a locket with a miniature of Mrs Fitzherbert's own eye, and her wedding ring which is a 'gimmel' with twin hoops — symbolic of lovers side by side — inscribed with the Prince's names

Plate 97 (top). The Marchionesss of Londonderry's ruby and emerald cross with enamelled flowers.

Plate 98 (above). The back of the Londonderry cross with Gothic revival tracery.

Plate 99 (*left*). Mrs Fitzherbert's diamond jewellery shown at the Exhibition of the Four Georges in London, 1931.

Plate 100 (*above*). Ring with miniature of King George IV by Henry Bone, presented to the Marchioness of Conygnham.

GEORGE AUGUSTUS FREDERICK. The most valuable of these most personal mementos is a locket with his miniature – not under glass or crystal but a flat picture diamond: his crowned cipher GP is at the back. The pair to it – with Mrs Fitzherbert's miniature – was found round his neck when George IV died in 1830: he had remained true to his youthful promise always to keep it next to his heart. These mementos, and Mrs Fitzherbert's diamond necklace, top and drop earrings and brooch with drop, were lent by the Countess of Portarlington to the Exhibition of the Four Georges held at 25 Park Lane in 1931 (Plate 99): they have not been exhibited since. More jewels were showered on the predatory Marchioness of Conyngham who supplanted Mrs Fitzherbert in the Prince's affections. At the Brighton Pavilion he and she spent hours looking at jewellery and, according to the memoirs of Charles Greville, 'she was chiefly intent on amassing money and collecting jewels'. It is said that two wagonloads of jewellery, plate etc. were sent away from Windsor Castle by Lady Conyngham as the King lay dying. Some of her plunder still remains in the family and those jewels that have been sold give a good idea of the quality of her collection: a miniature in a ring sold by Christie's on 28 July 1925 (Plate 100); a

locket crowned and framed with diamonds with the royal monogram on the back (Christie's, 15 June 1897); a diamond rivière (Sotheby's, 23 May 1985 – for £148,000); and the charming turquoise and diamond parure, now in a private collection (Plate 127).

King George IV took all the credit for the victory over the French at Waterloo and commissioned cameo portraits from Benedetto Pistrucci of himself triumphant in Roman armour and crowned with a laurel wreath. Two, mounted in lockets, are still in the Buccleuch and Devonshire collections. Also at Chatsworth is a portrait cameo – similarly imperial – in a hoop ring inscribed in bright Garter blue letters VIVE LE ROI (Long live the King); this is one of several made for the coronation of 1821. Much rarer, possibly unique, is the set of necklace, brooch and earrings given to Baroness Willoughby De Eresby, wife of the Lord Chamberlain, as a memento of the ceremony. Made by Rundell, Bridge and Rundell, they are inspired by the collar of a knight of the Garter and by the coronation regalia. The necklace consists of the emblems of shamrock, rose and thistle between the tasselled gold knots of the Garter collar with pendent orb surmounted by a Maltese cross. The orb, symbol of sovereignty, is repeated in the earrings and brooch (Plate 101).

Plate 101. Jewelled necklace with the emblems of England,
Scotland and Ireland between tasselled Garter collar knots, with
globe pendant: earrings and brooch en suite. The parure was
given to Baroness Willoughby De Eresby by King George IV on
his coronation in 1821.

Plate 102. Portrait of Viscount Harcourt holding the Prince of Wales's hat with diamond loop and button, painted by W. Hamilton.

Plate 103. The Harcourt family necklace. The largest stones and the pendant are from the hat loop and button given to Viscount Harcourt by the Prince of Wales after his wedding in 1795.

The French statesman Talleyrand admired King George IV's indifference to personal popularity and said he was the last king in the tradition of the *grands seigneurs*. Certainly he was master of the magnificent gesture. At his wedding to Princess Caroline of Brunswick-Wolfenbuttel in 1795, he asked George Simon second Viscount Harcourt, Master of the Horse, to hold his hat whose brim was pinned with a large diamond loop and button. After the ceremony in the Chapel Royal the Prince exchanged it for the Viscount's own hat, and its brooch of small value. In his portrait by William Hamilton, Harcourt holds the hat in his hand and at the back there is a note in his handwriting explaining how he came to possess it (Plate 102). The diamond button and loop are now in the centre of the Harcourt family necklace (Plate 103).

Queen Caroline

King George IV's marriage proved unhappy and his unfortunate wife Caroline was ignominiously turned away from Westminster Abbey when she tried to attend the coronation as was her right. Soon after, just before her death, she instituted an order for those who had stood by her. The Maltese cross she gave her lady-in-waiting Lady Anne Hamilton, one of those appointed to the order, has survived: it is set with amethysts and diamonds and each arm terminates in a crown. There is a long and pathetic inscription which begins with a reference to the crown: DENIED ON EARTH BESTOWID IN HEAVEN QUEEN CAROLINE OF BRUNSWICK ENGLAND'S INJURED QUEEN, and after the initials of the Queen and Lady Anne it continues in a facsimile of her handwriting,

I die in peace with all the world. Goodbye! Thank you my very dear Lady Anne for all your kindness to me, I cannot repay you. Do not regret me, my true friends ought not to weep for me. I shall be much happier in another world. I could only have known misery and persecution in this. They have destroyed me at last but their injured Queen forgives them. The doctors have done their best for me but they do not know my malady it is here ♥ but shall never come out of my lips: I am ready I

Plate 104. The cross of the Order of St Caroline sent to Lady Anne Hamilton by Queen Caroline just before she died in 1821.

am happy to die I have no wish to live. Remember me to my good friend Lady Perceval.

Until recently this cross was still in the collection of the Duke of Hamilton at Lennoxlove Castle (Plate 104).

Princess Charlotte

Queen Caroline was predeceased by her only daughter Princess Charlotte, who died in childbirth in 1817 aged twenty-one. In accordance with royal tradition Charlotte gave gifts of jewels to those close to her and her generosity occasionally caused financial embarrassment. Many were bracelets: in 1816, as godparents to Matilda, daughter of Admiral Strachan who served under Nelson at Trafalgar, the Princess and her husband Prince Leopold gave Lady Strachan a pair of inscribed bracelets. They were sold at Christie's on 15 December 1933 and were described in the catalogue as: 'formed of oblong gold plaques with shaped ends enamelled in colours each link bearing a letter to form the names Leopold and Charlotte in vari-coloured enamel. The central plaques are gold overlaid with green enamel in diamond borders and bear the letters L&C in diamonds with crowns above and swags of flowers below with single diamonds in each corner.' Other bracelets, given to Princess Charlotte's governess the Countess of Elgin, are composed of bright coloured stones – acquamarines, amethysts, turquoises, opals, garnets and topazes. These were sold at Sotheby's on 8 May 1986.

William IV and Queen Adelaide

Jewels which King William IV and Queen Adelaide gave his daughters by the vivacious actress Mrs Jordan, the Fitzclarences, have an unmistakably royal character. Lady Elizabeth Fitzclarence's bracelet clasps – which can also be worn as brooches – are Tudor roses enclosing the royal ciphers WR and AR on blue enamel; inherited by her daughter Lady Ida Hay, they are still in the collection of her descendant the Earl of Gainsborough. Queen Adelaide left another pair of these bracelets – with diamond rings – to Lady Augusta Fitzclarence. These were sold, with the diamond tiara of Madonna lilies given on her marriage to Mr William Kennedy Erskine of Dun in July 1836, by their descendants at Christie's on 7 June 1944 (Plate 105). Miniatures of the King and Queen may also have a Fitzclarence provenance, one being the locket described in Christie's catalogue for a sale held on 23 June 1947: 'enriched with six diamonds with a single diamond above on a square blue enamel and gold plaque and a similar pendant containing enamelled portraits of King William IV and Queen Adelaide in a border inscribed THE LAST

GIFT OF MY BELOVED GRANDFATHER KING WILLIAM IV.' The Tudor rose ornaments were gifts the Queen made to her own friends; for example the gold and enamel bracelet composed of a rose with matted gold petals and turned over tips: in the centre is a miniature of a lady in court dress with pearls in her hair forming stamens. The gold hinged band is enamelled with sprays of forget-me-nots on a matted ground and inscribed inside GIVEN BY QUEEN ADELAIDE QUEEN CONSORT OF ENGLAND TO EMILY MARCHIONESS OF WEST MEATH AND LEFT BY HER AS AN HEIRLOOM IN THE FAMILY OF LADY ROSE GREVILLE. It was sold by Lord Greville at Christie's on 7 December 1960. Marchioness Emily, who had been Lady of the Bedchamber to Queen Adelaide, died at St James's Palace in 1858.

Plate 105 (*below*). The Fitzclarence bracelets with Tudor rose clasps with diamond ciphers of King William IV and Queen Adelaide on blue enamel.

Plate 106 (*right*). The Bedford tiara, bought by the sixth Duke from ex-Queen Caroline of Naples. It is set in the Napoleonic style with gems engraved with classical motifs.

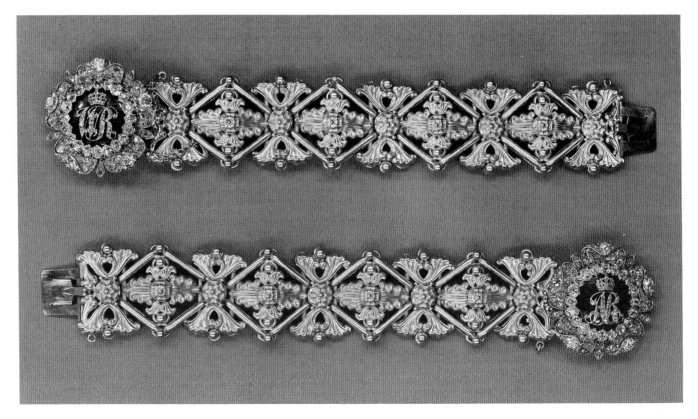

Napoleonic Jewellery

Members of the *ancien régime* impoverished by the Revolution had been obliged to sell jewellery in London and the Bonaparte family had to do the same after the collapse of the First Empire. When Joseph Bonaparte abdicated from the throne of Spain in 1813 he took with him the famous Pelegrina pearl from the Spanish crown jewels which he bequeathed to Prince Louis Napoleon who sold it to the then Marquis of Hamilton, later first Duke of Abercorn. Pear-shaped and weighing 58½ carats, it has been depicted in state portraits of the Queens of Spain since the early seventeenth century. Lord Frederic Hamilton, in his autobiography, *Here There and Everywhere* (1921), remembered his mother did not always enjoy wearing this historic object:

To my mother it was an unceasing source of anxiety. The pearl had never been bored, and was so heavy that it was constantly falling from its setting. Three times she lost it; three times she found it again. Once at a ball at Buckingham Palace, on putting her hand to her neck, she found that the great pearl had gone. She was much distressed, knowing how upset my father would be. On going into supper, she saw '*La Pelegrina*' gleaming at her from the folds of the velvet train of the lady immediately in front of her. Again she lost it at Windsor Castle, and it was found in the upholstery of a sofa. . . . When it came into my brother's possession after my father's death, he had '*La Pelegrina*' bored, though it impaired its value, so my sister-in-law was able to wear the great jewel as often as she wished without running the constant danger of losing it.

During World War I the Duchess of Abercorn tried to sell the Pelegrina for £35,000 through the jewellers Hennell. Photographs of it mounted in diamond leaves and worn by the Duchesses of Abercorn were sent to rich Americans such as Judge Geary the steel magnate, and in 1917 to Mrs Henry Huntingdon. Most recently Richard Burton acquired it at a sale at Sotheby Parke Bernet on 23 January 1969 and gave it to Miss Elizabeth Taylor.

Under Napoleon a version of neo-classical art inspired by imperial Rome was employed to glorify his empire. As the jewels of the empresses of antiquity had been set with cameos and intaglios so also were the ornaments of the women of the Bonaparte family, richly framed in pearls and precious stones. Thus the tiara of Queen Caroline of Naples, bought by the sixth Duke of Bedford in 1817, is set with nine nicolo (onyx of blue and black layers) intaglios depicting the heroes and divinities of mythology with pearl clusters between (Plate 106). The 'ceinture Gothique' made by N.E. Nitot of Paris which Napoleon's second Empress, the Austrian Archduchess Marie-Louise, wore with her wedding dress in 1810 is likewise lavishly embellished with pearls and the buckle is set with a cameo of Apollo. The ex-Empress bequeathed it in 1848 — with the emerald ring she always wore on her right hand and a bonbonnière — to her friend Priscilla, wife of the eleventh Earl of Westmorland. Lady Westmorland was the niece of Napoleon's conqueror, the Duke of Wellington: her husband was a diplomat who served at the courts of Florence and in Parma, where the ex-Express lived. The belt was sold by their daughter Lady Rose Weigall at the end of the last century; it appeared most recently at auction at Christie's on 8 May 1985.

Cameos and Intaglios

Other British women adopted the Napoleonic fashion for jewels with engraved gems. The Countess of Elgin told her mother about the beautiful cameo she bought in 1803: 'You have no idea how much it was esteemed in Rome, the artists used to come and look at it.' The very rich Charlotte Florentia, wife of the third Duke of Northumberland, had a complete parure set with cameo portraits: five brooches, earrings and necklace, all in blue enamelled gold linked by pearl swags. She wore it to the historic ball held by the Duchess of Richmond in Brussels on the eve of the Battle of Waterloo. Bequeathed to her niece Henrietta Williams of Bodelwyddan, it was sold by her son Major Peel at Christie's on 14 July 1948.

The Northumberland hardstone cameo parure was unusual, for most were set with shell cameos which were softer and easier to carve. Duchess Charlotte, wife of the fifth Duke of Buccleuch and Queensberry, had one of these, consisting of necklace, bracelets and earrings, mounted in showy gold scrollwork. It was sold by Christie's on 8 July 1940. The shell cameo comb and belt buckle bought in Rome while on the Grand Tour by Lord Charles Murray for his mother, second wife of the fourth Duke of Atholl, is still at Blair Castle. The two cameos on the buckle represent night and day, after the reliefs by the celebrated Danish sculptor Bertel Thorwaldsen, much admired at the time for their poetic quality. The comb is surmounted by a version of the famous ancient fresco called the Aldobrandini marriage, found on the Esquiline in 1604 and acquired by Cardinal

Cinto Aldobrandini before entering the Vatican collections in 1818. It represents the preparations for a wedding with gods and goddesses seated beside mortals while musicians and handmaidens perform sacred rites (Plate 107).

Shell cameo carvers specialised in portraiture as well as miniature versions of contemporary and ancient monuments. Giuseppe Dies, who got a good likeness, was the favourite of most English travellers, and his portraits of the eighth Duke of Bedford and his wife Anna Maria set in pearl and diamond pendants are preserved at Woburn Abbey. The clasp of a bracelet copied from a Roman model found at Pompeii is set with a shell cameo bust of the young Eliza Ellice who accompanied her parents, General Robert Ellice and his wife Eliza, to Italy in 1825. In 1838 Eliza married Henry Brand, future Speaker of the House of Commons and first Viscount Hampden, and the bracelet is still at their home Glynde Place in East Sussex (Plate 108).

Trophies of War

After the victory of the Nile in 1798 Sultan Selim III gave Viscount Nelson a diamond 'chelengk' or plume of triumph. The thirteen diamond spikes radiating upwards represented the enemy ships destroyed in the battle. It was the first ever awarded to a Christian, and Nelson proudly incorporated it into his coat of arms. It descended with the viscountcy of Nelson and dukedom of Bronte for several generations until acquired by the National Maritime Museum, from whom it was stolen in 1951. In 1801 the Sultan gave a second chelengk to Admiral Viscount Keith, Commander in Chief of the Mediterranean Fleet, and appointed him to the Order of the Crescent. The diamond star of the Order, the chelengk, and another gift — a chatelaine and watch decorated with a dia-

Plate 107 (*top*). Three shell cameos: the Aldobrandini marriage, set in a comb, and Night and Day, after the reliefs by Bertel Thorwaldsen, set in a belt clasp, bought in Rome by Lord Charles Murray in 1823.

Plate 108 (*right*). Pompeian-style bracelet with shell cameo profile of Eliza Ellice, later Viscountess Hampden.

mond picture of Constantinople – were inherited by Viscount Keith's granddaughter Emily who married the fourth Marquess of Landsdowne in 1843. While on display at Bowood in Wiltshire the star and chelengk were stolen: they have been replaced with replicas.

The jewelled insignia of the European orders of chivalry presented to the Duke of Wellington after the victory of Waterloo were enshrined at Apsley House. Some were very valuable: two diamonds in the badge of the Order of the Saint Esprit, to which the Duke was appointed by Louis XVII, were valued at £25,000. They could be traced back to Louis XIV and Napoleon wore them in the quillions of his sword. After the abolition of the Order in 1830 they were reset as a pair of earrings for the future second Duchess, then Marchioness of Douro.

Anglo-Indian Jewellery

Those who served with the Indian army or administration continued to acquire gems and jewellery there. There was widespread plunder after the storming of the cruel and despotic Tippoo Sahib's stronghold of Seringapatam in 1799, and British officers shared the loot: a large sapphire from Tippoo Sahib's sword hilt was subsequently worn in a ring (sold at Christie's on 9 June 1892) and his four-row pearl necklace was given by Sir John Floyd – in charge of the army – to his daughter Julia, wife of Sir Robert Peel, twice Prime Minister to Queen Victoria. This was sold by Christie's on 3 February 1917.

Elaborate diamond, ruby, emerald and pearl Indian necklaces were brought home by Lord Amherst of Arracan, Governor General of India 1823-8; the backs of the settings were just as bright with red and green Jaipur enamel – a typically oriental combination of colours. They were sold by Christie's on 12 June 1929.

Bridal Parures

As in the eighteenth century, new parures were made for noble marriages. The Temple diamonds given to Lady Anne Brydges, heiress to the third and last Duke of Chandos, in 1796 on her marriage to

Richard Temple, later first Duke of Buckingham, survived into this century. Her mother had proposed the marriage in 1786 when the couple were very young – he ten, and she six. The diamond parure consisted of a rivière of forty-three graduated stones, matching chains of oval links – making two necklaces and a pair of bracelets – three pins for the hair and bodice and a large spray of roses and thistles. In spite of huge financial losses which necessitated the sale of most of the library and art treasures at the family home of Stowe the nineteenth-century Dukes of Buckingham held fast to the Temple diamonds, and they are mentioned as heirlooms in the will of the third Duke in 1889. They were sold by his daughter at Christie's on 12 June 1929 (Plate 244).

Even by the lavish standards of the day the jewels which the fifth Duke of Buccleuch and Queensberry gave Lady Charlotte Thynne at the time of their marriage in 1829 were particularly splendid. The bride's mother, the Marchioness of Bath, mentioned them proudly to her friend, the novelist the Hon. Emily Eden. Together they 'went poking over the house looking for presents he had given her. Such quantities of pretty things...the jewels were not finished...the diamonds and emeralds will be superb, Lady Bath said, but I think the pearls the handsomest set I ever saw.' As the Duke continued to add to her collection throughout their long life together (he died in 1884) the Buccleuch jewels, and above all the spectacular diamond belt (Plate 211), always provided a talking point whenever the Duchess appeared in them, and have continued to do so.

Jewels for the Hair

Birds, butterflies, feathers, stars and crescents remained in fashion, and wreaths of flowers – wild roses and Jasmine (Plates 109 and 110), daisies (Plates 111 and 112), fuschias (Plates 113 and 114) and lilies encircled the head as tiaras. The Marlborough diamonds were reset in a neo-classical bandeau of Greek fret and honeysuckles for Countess Spencer: it is still in the family (Plates 115, 116 and 117). The oak leaf, with its patriotic associations was adopted for diamond wreaths celebrating the victories of Trafalgar and Waterloo (Plate 118).

Plate 109. The Bedford diamond tiara of jasmine and wild roses in the style of the Romantic period.

Plate 110. The Marchioness of Tavistock with the Bedford tiara and necklace in 1980.

Plate 111. Lady Lucy Primrose wearing the Rosebery tiara over her wedding veil.

Plate 112. The Rosebery family diamond tiara of daisies; it is a Primrose heirloom.

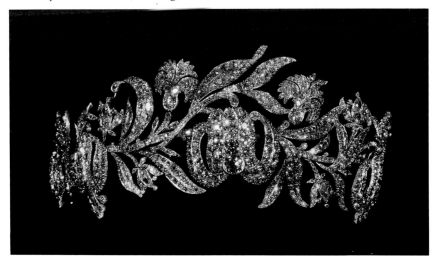

Plate 113. The Rutland diamond botanical tiara, shown at the Exhibition of the Four Georges in 1931.

Plate 114. The Dowager Duchess of Rutland wearing the family tiara in 1959.

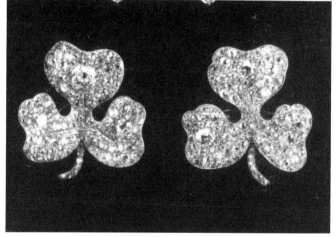

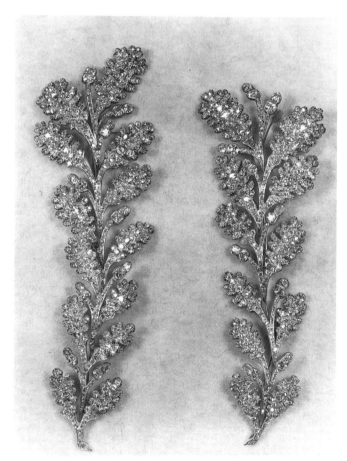

Plate 118 (*above*). Twin sprays of oak leaves, worn in a wreath on the head.

Plate 115 (*top left*). The Spencer diamond tiara with classical-style honeysuckle and Greek fret: it was shown at the Exhibition of the Four Georges in 1931.

Plate 116 (*top middle*). Countess Charlotte, wife of the fifth Earl Spencer, wearing the Spencer honeysuckle tiara in 1885.

Plate 119 (*above*). The Shrewsbury diamond shamrocks commissioned by Maria Theresa, wife of the sixteenth Earl.

Plate 120 (*left*). Nadine, Countess of Shrewsbury, wife of the twenty-first Earl, wearing the diamond shamrocks with floral sprigs in her hair at a ball in London in 1955.

Plate 117 (*top right*). Countess Cynthia, wife of the seventh Earl Spencer, photographed by Lenare in 1953. She is wearing the family honeysuckle tiara with her robes for the coronation of Queen Elizabeth II.

Earrings

The theme of triumph was repeated in earrings of oak and laurel (Plate 121) such as the pair sold by the Hon. Mrs Arthur Crichton at Christie's on 20 June 1921 and described in the catalogue as 'a pair of Old English diamond pendants each composed of an oval diamond drop supported by a three-stone diamond chain to diamond leaves which hold a flexible frame of graduated diamonds with diamond cluster top'. An excellent example of the top and drop style was given by Mrs Fitzherbert to her niece Charlotte Smythe — whom the Duke of Orléans called the prettiest girl in England — for her marriage to the Hon. George Augustus Craven in 1833: here the pear-shaped drops swing from clusters (Plate 122). They were sold by Sotheby's on 30 November 1961. Drops of coloured stones were also thought becoming. Lady Elizabeth Coke, who asked her future husband John Spencer Stanhope of Cannon Hall, Yorkshire for a pair of pale green chrysoprase earrings when they married in 1822, explained, 'earrings are the only things I care much about being rather vain of my ears'. A more expensive pair of the same date is still in the Exeter collection at Burghley House: the long emerald drops swing between double chains of finely worked gold.

Necklaces

In addition to simple clusters and rivières the Georgians were fond of elaborate designs with festoons and fringes. The festoon style is illustrated by the emerald and diamond necklace bought by the Devonshire landowner and MP Sir Thomas Dyke Acland for his wife Lydia in 1815 and sold by their great-great-grandson at Sotheby's on 26 June 1973 (Plate 123). Festoons also hang from the diamond

Plate 121 (*top*). Diamond earrings and brooch with sprays of oak leaves.

Plate 122 (*middle*). Diamond earrings given by Mrs Fitzherbert to her niece, the Hon. Mrs George Craven, in 1833.

Plate 123 (*right*). The Acland family diamond and emerald necklace, bought by Sir Thomas Dyke Acland in 1815.

cluster necklace worn by the Countess of Shrewsbury to the coronation of William IV in 1831 (Plate 124). This was sold by Sotheby's on 18 February 1960. It can be seen in her portrait, where she is posed against the Gothic architecture of Westminster Abbey (Plate 125).

Until recently the Marquess of Anglesey owned an unusual diamond necklace called a negligeé. The three rows of stones were not fastened by a clasp but ended in twin tassels. It can be seen thrown round the neck of the Marchioness of Anglesey in a photograph by Cecil Beaton taken at the time of the coronation of 1937 (Plate 126), and was lent to the Ageless Diamond exhibition held at Christie's in 1959: it is no longer in the family.

Plate 126. The Marchioness of Anglesey photographed by Cecil Beaton dressed for the coronation of King George VI in 1937 and wearing the family diamond negligeé.

Plate 124. The Shrewsbury diamond cluster necklace fringed with festoons and pendants.

Plate 125 (*left*). Maria Theresa, wife of the sixteenth Earl of Shrewsbury, wearing the family diamond necklace with her robes for the coronation of King William IV in a portrait by J.K. Hamburger.

Turquoises were the favourite semi-precious stones: the Marchioness of Londonderry asked to be buried with her turquoise rings, and the Marchioness of Conyngham wore them in a parure, highlighted with diamonds (Plate 127). The turquoise and diamond cluster necklace of Clementina, wife of the twenty-first Baron Willoughby De Eresby, is still worn today by the present Baroness with the Drummond plaid (Plate 134). Turquoises contrast dramatically with large pieces of jasper in filigree borders linked by gold chains in a necklace, bracelet and pendent brooch (Plate 128), still in the box with other jewellery taken to Australia by the original owner in the early 1850s. Her husband suffered from asthma and on doctor's orders they went to Tasmania in the hope that the dry climate might cure him. In

Plate 127. Turquoise and diamond parure given by King George
IV to the Marchioness of Conyngham.

Plate 128. Jasper and turquoise necklace, brooch and bracelet
c. 1830.

the event it was the wife who died there and her young children brought her jewels home to England. They are now in a noble north country collection (Plate 129).

Plate 129. The suite shown in Plate 128, here photographed with other jewels in the original box as taken to Australia and back in the 1850s.

Crosses

The cross which so often hung as a pendant to necklaces might be set with diamonds or coloured stones, both precious and semi-precious. A fine example belonged to the Nottingham heiress Esther Acklom, who married the future third Earl Spencer in 1814. Eight very white brilliants placed at each extremity and between the arms enhance the colour of five long bright green emeralds. This cross is still in the Spencer collection: in 1960 it was lent to the exhibition of jewellery held in Birmingham. Echoing the crosses on the royal crown and perhaps alluding to the island of Malta coming under British sovereignty in 1797, the Maltese design was liked because good stones showed to advantage at the ends of the wide arms.

Brooches

The ideal place to display ancestral stones was in the brooch pinned to the centre of the neckline, called a sévigné, after the famous letter writer at the court of Louis XIV, who wears one in a portrait. One of the most spectacular was until recently owned by the Dukes of Northumberland. It is set with an enormous beautiful dark green emerald carved with foliage in the Mughal style introduced into India in the

Plate 130. The Northumberland pendant set with carved Mughal emerald framed in diamonds with emerald drop, worn by Duchess Charlotte Florentia, wife of the third Duke, as Vicereine of Ireland 1828–9. She inherited it from her grandfather Baron Clive of Plassey, or from her father who also served as Governor-General of India.

Plate 131. Pansy brooch set with amethysts, topazes, chrysoprases and diamonds. A gift to the Countess of Listowel in 1810, it then passed through two more generations.

seventeenth century through the patronage of Shah Jehan, builder of the Taj Mahal. Duchess Charlotte Florentia, wife of the third Duke, had it set in diamond foliage and hung with a smaller emerald as a drop by Rundell, Bridge and Rundell in 1829 when her husband was appointed Viceroy of Ireland (Plate 130). It must have been acquired in India by her grandfather the famous Robert Clive, or by her father the second Baron Clive of Plassey, both of whom were Governors-General. Norman Hartnell, the royal dressmaker, has described the effect of this brooch when it was worn by Helen Duchess of Northumberland, Mistress of the Robes to Queen Elizabeth, the wife of King George VI: 'in an evening dress of lily-like beauty perfectly suited to her slender height, and among her jewels a most magnificent stomacher or pendulous ornament of an inch-square emerald'. The brooch was sold by her son at Sotheby's on 4 April 1978, where it fetched £250,000.

Flower brooches were often symbolic, and a favourite was the pansy with its message 'Remember me'. An attractive pansy brooch, the petals set with amethysts and topazes, the stamens with diamonds and chrysoprases, which passed through three generations of an Irish family, has its history inscribed on the back of the petals. It begins with ANNE LATHOM COUNTESS OF LISTOWEL 1810, followed by her stepson WILLIAM THIRD EARL OF BANTRY and ends with the name of his eldest surviving daughter OLIVIA LADY ARDILAUN. This is now in a London private collection (Plate 131).

Bracelets

Bracelets were worn prominently on the wrists, sometimes in rows right up to the elbow (Plate 133). The clasp was usually massive with a fine stone — Brazilian topaz, amethyst, chrysoprase — in the centre framed in richly chased gold, alloyed in different colours. A large acquamarine in a bracelet of around 1830 is guarded by two knights in armour standing in crocketed niches: made for Lady Anne Lindsay Crawford it reflects the Romantic influence of Sir Walter Scott's historical novels (Plate 132). It is in a noble Scottish collection.

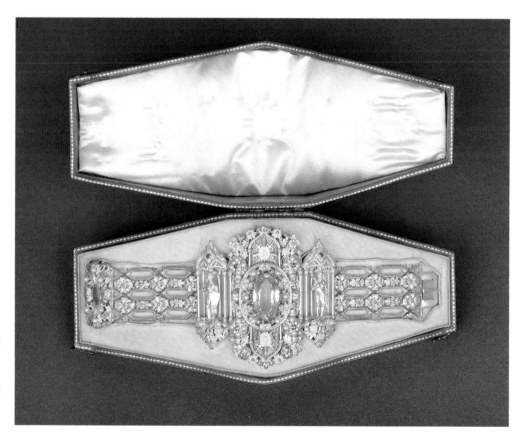

Plate 132 (*right*). Bracelet with large acquamarine guarded by two knights standing in crocketed niches, reflecting the influence of Sir Walter Scott's historical novels.

Most bracelets express sentiment: the clasps or bands might be jewelled with stones whose initials spelt out messages such as REGARD or DEAREST, christian names and anniversaries. Some represent the snake, symbol of eternity, and others the hand, clasped in love and friendship. Reminding the wearer of the donor every time she glanced down at her wrist, bracelets made ideal keepsakes.

Rings

Like bracelets, rings were worn in quantities: portraits show several on one finger, right up to the knuckle (Plate 133). Unfortunately we seldom know the provenance of gem-set rings, and for this reason it is of great interest that at Drummond Castle in Scotland there is a group of turquoise rings which must have belonged to Clementina Baroness Willoughby De Eresby: they are in the same box as her necklace (Plate 134). At Althorp, the home of the Spencers, there was for many years a 'gimmel' ring inscribed MEG SEYMOUR ER DE MONTALEMBERT PARIS 13 JUNE 1823. It is made in the shape of clasped hands – the motif also found in bracelets – and is a memento of the friendship between Mrs Fitzherbert's adopted daughter Minnie Seymour – connected with the family by marriage – and Elise Rose, wife of the French Royalist soldier and historian, Marc René de Montalembert. It was sold by S.J. Phillips in 1978.

Plate 133 (*left*). Portrait of Lady Peel by Sir Thomas Lawrence. The feathers in her black velvet hat are pinned with an amethyst cluster brooch.

Plate 134 (*right*). Clementina Baroness Willoughby De Eresby's jewel box containing her turquoise and diamond cluster necklace and her rings, *c.* 1820.

Children's Jewellery

Children's rings have a particular charm. Three little ones formerly in the Spencer collection are miniature versions of adult styles, two set with turquoises, and the third a blue enamelled snake. They were sold by S.J. Phillips in 1978. At Blair Castle the family still has the coral necklace of grooved round beads which was worn by their ancestor the sixth Duke of Atholl as a child around 1800.

Although the gift has long gone, the old-world sentiment of the verses which accompanied a watch given to the infant future fifth Marquess of Londonderry still survives:

> Dear beauteous boy whose infant years proclaim
> The rising greatness for your future fame,
> Take from a friend whose name you scarcely know
> A gift which few so early would bestow.
> Take it – sweet boy – I know your opening mind
> Ere long its moral usefulness will find
> And when you've learnt from it to value time
> Forget not him who penned this humble rhyme!

Memorial Jewellery

The large ruby and diamond locket which a Welsh heiress, Mrs Lucy of Charlecote in Warwickshire, hung from her necklace when she was presented at the court of King George IV is likely to have contained a lock of hair hidden inside it, or set under glass in front and decoratively framed like a picture. There are lockets in both styles at Grimsthorpe Castle. One is a heart with a turquoise and pearl forget-me-not on the gold cover which opens up to show the hair inside, under glass, and the other has a Gothic frame studded with rubies and emeralds. A large symbolic heart in blue enamel at Glynde Place, East Sussex, is a memorial to the love affair between Georgiana Duchess of Devonshire and the second Earl Grey, famous for his introduction of the Reform Bill of 1832. It contains intertwined locks of their hair, their initials in gold letters on the glass, and the inscription IL M'EST FIDEL (Plate 135). Their daughter Eliza Courtney, who was born in 1792, kept this memento of her parents

Plate 135. Heart-shaped locket enclosing the hair of Georgiana Duchess of Devonshire and of the future Earl Grey.

Plate 136. Their granddaughter Viscountess Hampden, wearing the Devonshire-Grey love token.

and left it to her own daughter, also Eliza, wife of the first Viscount Hampden. She wears it high on the neck in a portrait which is also at Glynde Place (Plate 136).

During the wave of patriotism which swept the country in the long years of war against the French the hair of military and naval heroes was prized, and set in jewels like reliquaries. Lady Neville, for instance, wore a brooch containing a lock of hair which the Viscount Nelson (created Duke of Bronte in 1801) had given her husband, an officer on the flagship *Victory*: it bore the crowned initials N(elson) and B (ronte) and the inscription LOST TO HIS COUNTRY OCT 21 1805. It was sold by Christie's on 6 February 1935.

Court mourning was most strictly observed and a gold chain bracelet at Grimsthorpe Castle recalls the universal grief at the premature death of Princess Charlotte, only child of the Prince Regent. The clasp is inscribed BORN 7 JAN 1796 DIED 6 NOV 1817, and the lock of hair — set under glass — is encircled by a snake, tail in mouth, symbolic of love which

would endure beyond the grave. It was worn by her friend Baroness Willoughby De Eresby.

Interest in the Stuarts was renewed by the unexpected discovery of the coffin of King Charles I in St George's Chapel at Windsor. A lock of his hair is at Grimsthorpe Castle, under glass, in a crowned brooch framed in a buckled Garter. The back is inscribed KING CHARLES IST HAIR TAKEN OUT OF THE VAULT AT WINDSOR MARCH 31ST 1813 GIVEN BY SIR H(enr)Y HOLFORD TO THE PRINCESS CHARLOTTE AND BY HRH TO THE LADY WILLOUGHBY D'ERESBY (Plates 137 and 138).

Ornaments made from the hair of the children and grandchildren of the Dukes of Atholl are still at Blair Castle: among these are two snakes, woven from the hair of Lady Harriet and Lord Charles Murray, and a wide band braided from the hair of James Charles Plantagenet Murray, the clasp inscribed with his initials and birthday, 8 DEC 1820, and set with a shell cameo of Cupid captive. Mourning bracelets of this type were worn in memory of Georgiana

Plate 137. Crowned Garter brooch containing the hair of King Charles I, given to Baroness Willoughby De Eresby in 1813.

Plate 138. The back of the Garter brooch, inscribed with its history.

Duchess of Devonshire who died in 1806. They were fastened with onyx clasps inscribed with the date and the initials GD. Only a ring containing her hair, inscribed SOEUR ET AMIE (Sister and friend), with the ducal coronet, initials and diamond snakes – the Cavendish badge – survives at Chatsworth: it could have been worn by her sister the Countess of Bessborough, and was returned to the family. In the Devonshire collection there is a most interesting bracelet, worn by Princess Pauline Borghese in mourning for her brother Napoleon after his death in 1821, and which she sent to the sixth Duke of Devonshire to cover a break in the arm of Bertel Thorwaldsen's statue of Venus damaged in the journey to Derbyshire from Rome. She and the Duke became friends while he was in Rome buying works of art, and he enjoyed her conversation, 'when not compelled to talk about dress'. The bracelet is enamelled with black scrolls and inscribed ROMA 23 APRILE 1824 (Plate 139).

Even more common were memorial rings. Some are very moving, particularly those for children. The brief life of Catherine Stanhope, who died aged five, was recalled by two pathetic mementos at Cannon Hall in Yorkshire: a lock of her hair labelled MY DEAR LITTLE CATHERINE'S HAIR CUT OFF THE MORNING I LOST HER, NOVEMBER 20TH, 1795, and the large ring which never left her mother's finger until her own death. Those remaining in other families bring to mind a medley of historical characters. At Burghley House, Dr Willis, responsible for George III during his years of madness, is remembered by a black ring with a forget-me-not on the bezel, General Paoli the Corsican general and patriot who died in exile aged eighty-two in London by a ring at Lennoxlove, and Nathan Meyer de Rothschild, founder of the British branch of the banking dynasty and its financial genius, by a gold snake ring worn by his granddaughter the Countess of Rosebery. The inscription IN MEMORY OF NM DE ROTHSCHILD OB 28 JULY 1836 is inside the hoop.

Plate 139. The bracelet which Princess Pauline Borghese gave the sixth Duke of Devonshire. She wore it in mourning for her brother the Emperor Napoleon.

Fancy-coloured diamond tiara of scroll and foliate design.

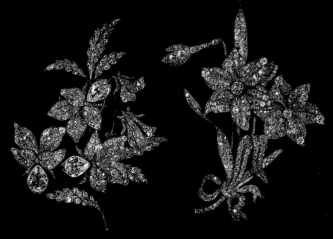

Two diamond floral sprays bought from Tessier of Bond Street, London, *c.* 1840.

Diamond rivière.

Double row of pearls with diamond clasp, bought from Robert Garrard of London in 1843 for £886, an enormous sum for those days.

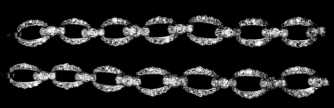

Pair of diamond chain link bracelets.

Sapphire in diamond scroll frame with pear pearl pendant.

Five
THE VICTORIANS

A full and happy domestic life did not prevent the young Queen Victoria fulfilling her official duties. She gave a spirited lead to her court and the costume ball held at Buckingham Palace in 1842 to encourage the luxury trades gave a pretext for wearing more jewels than were usually seen. Guests came dressed as the persons from the past whom they most admired. The Queen and Prince Albert were attired as Queen Philippa and Edward III, and the Duchess of Cambridge led a procession in Plantagenet court dress. Released from their obligatory black coats, the men rose to the occasion. Lord Pembroke, as François I, hired £10,000 worth of diamonds for the night from Storr & Mortimer at a fee of 1 per cent, and the Duke of Devonshire, who came as Queen Elizabeth's favourite the Earl of Leicester, wore his Garter star on a violet doublet with more diamonds flashing out from the hilt of his sword. A glowing account of the picturesque scene appeared in the *Illustrated London News*: 'noblemen and noble ladies wore diamonds and precious ornaments to the amount of many thousands…and when one considers the vast treasures of jewels descending as heirlooms in hereditary line from our proud and ancient aristocratic houses we cannot wonder that this fête was acknowledged by all present to surpass those of every other country'. So enjoyable were these occasions that many of those present held their own costume balls the following year.

At her next ball in 1845 the Queen's guests came in the costume of the period 1740-50, and in powdered hair, patches and wigs danced old English gavottes, minuets and the Sir Roger de Coverley in the Palace picture gallery. The *Illustrated London News* described the stately Marchioness of Douro,

her petticoat of white brocade with gold, a flounce of the most valuable point lace formerly belonging to the Popes of Rome. Her dress was of splendid brocade with silver, the front being open and ornamented with silver bullion and rosettes of diamonds, and the stomacher most superbly covered with diamonds. Each sleeve was ornamented with diamonds in the form of coronets and trimmed with point lace to match the flounce, her headdress was a coronet of diamonds and rubies, and her shoes of white satin were trimmed with red ribbon, a rosette on each with a large diamond in the centre. Her ladyship carried a magnificent antique fan decorated with rubies. The value of the diamonds and jewels worn by her ladyship amounted to £60,000. Her necklace of pearls, rubies and diamonds was fastened on black velvet with bracelets to match.

More family jewels adorned the Marchioness's father-in-law the Duke of Wellington, who looked splendid as a field marshal carrying a rich sword with emerald and diamond hilt and the fabulous diamond badge of the Golden Fleece given him by the Bourbon Countess of Chinchón after the success of his Spanish campaign. The badge was stolen from Apsley House in 1965 and has never been recovered (Plate 268).

Plate 140. Lady Middleton, painted by F.X. Winterhalter in 1863.
Her diamond necklace, the stars in her hair, emerald bracelet and
rings were broken up and dispersed after her death in 1901.

Plate 141. Gold hawk badge of the hereditary Grand Falconer of England, the Duke of St Albans, worn on a green velvet suit to the costume ball held at Buckingham Palace in 1845.

Plate 142 (*below*). The Duchess of St Albans in eighteenth-century dress at the costume ball at Buckingham Palace in 1845.

Plate 143 (*opposite, top*). Diamond hawk which the Duchess of Albans wore on her dress pictured in Plate 142.

Plate 144 (*opposite, below*). The Duke and Duchess of St Albans in seventeenth-century costume on horseback with falcons, drawn by Edward Thomas Parris in 1840.

The ninth Duke of St Albans came dressed as Hereditary Grand Falconer — the office awarded his ancestor, the first Duke, son of King Charles II and Nell Gwynne. His badge, a large gold hawk on a perch within a circle, hung from a massive gold chain fastened by a Tudor rose clasp (Plate 141): he wore it over a rich emerald green velvet coat lined with white satin trimmed with gold lace and fastened with gold buttons. His Duchess Elizabeth (Plate 142), according to The *Illustrated London News*, was elegant in

a tunic and bodice of violet satin brocaded in brilliant silver flowers: the tunic looped up with garlands of red and white roses, the bodice square and tight fitting, the stomacher of white satin covered with silver point lace, three rows of ruffles of similar silver lace on the sleeves, an upper skirt of white satin trimmed with a deep flounce of point de Bayeux looped up in festoons of deep rose colour. The rose-coloured satin underskirt trimmed with magnificent flounces of silver lace was headed by quiltings of rose coloured ribbon. She wore a little green velvet Pompadour hat with rose coloured feathers, diamond tiara, hair powdered and dressed in ringlets à la Louis XV ornamented with pearls and a diamond stomacher and the hawk on her left shoulder.

COSTUME OF HER GRACE THE DUCHESS OF ST. ALBANS.

This hawk – also in an open circle – is entirely paved with brilliant-cut diamonds with a gold collar and claws (Plate 143). Both the gold and the diamond hawk are still in the possession of the Duke of St Albans.

The Queen gave a third ball for the Great Exhibition of 1851, when the guests were invited to come dressed as courtiers from the reign of Louis XIV and King Charles II. This too was a success, but it was overshadowed by the Exhibition itself. Among the many English firms who put their wares on display were the principal London jewellers – Emanuel, Hunt and Roskell, Howell and James, and Robert Garrard. They, with other firms, made their international reputations at the exhibitions which followed – Paris in 1862, 1878, 1889, Vienna in 1873, Philadelphia in 1875 and Chicago in 1893 – where their stands were showcases for a rather solid style of jewellery more remarkable for the beauty of the stones than for elegant design. It was the taste of their aristocratic clients who were benefiting from a period of national prosperity. The political climate was stable, taxation was low, efficient domestic service was cheap and the nation wealthier than ever through the Industrial Revolution and imperial power.

The great families still held court in their country estates, and Disraeli described the scene at Belvoir Castle in 1850: 'We live in the state rooms brilliantly illuminated at night and at all times deliciously warm even in this severe winter. A military band plays while we are at dinner and occasionally throughout the evening. Dinner is announced to the air of the "Roast Beef of Old England"...Almost all the gentlemen being members of the famous Belvoir Hunt which adds greatly to the gaiety and brilliancy of the scene.' Mary Boyle stayed at Burghley House and admired 'the spacious rooms whose walls were decorated with pictures of old Italian masters profusely lighted, groups of gaily dressed and richly jewelled ladies enlivened by a sprinkling of Knights of the Bath and of the Garter, with numbers of male attendants in the traditional garb of the retainers of the house of Cecil in sky blue livery resplendent with frogs and aiguillettes of silver.'

The grand and feudal atmosphere at Haddo House in Scotland is captured in Edward Emslie's group

Plate 145. A dinner given by the Marquess and Marchioness of Aberdeen in honour of the Prime Minister, Mr Gladstone, at Haddo House in Aberdeenshire, painted by Alfred Edward Emslie in 1884.

portrait of a dinner party given by the first Marquess of Aberdeen in honour of Mr Gladstone in 1884. Wax candles in silver candelabra light the table laden with priceless china and rare fruits while the piper Andrew Cant walks round the room playing the bagpipes (Plate 145).

In this era of confidence and prosperity jewels — always a sign of rank — were worn in greater quantities than ever before. A woman with a busy social life and a large wardrobe needed more than one parure, as Mrs Gore explained in her novel *A Lady of Fashion* (1856): 'I cannot always be sparkling in diamonds. I must have emeralds for one style of dress, and sapphires for another — no leader of bon ton can get on without all sorts and sizes of pretty gems.' They were the most important part of a bridal trousseau and on getting engaged a man would go through his family jewels and have them brought up to date — often with the addition of new stones — for his future wife. In 1876, for instance, the bride of

the Earl of Clarendon wore his gift of a diamond parure — tiara, necklace, stomacher, bracelet and pendant — for the first time with her wedding dress, as did Miss Alberta Victoria Paget when she married Lord Windsor in 1883. Other jewels were given by wealthy friends and from tenants whose subscriptions raised substantial sums. As the century drew to an end ancient jewel caskets were increasingly replenished by marriages with the daughters of the captains of industry and finance, and also with American heiresses. Cornelia Bradley Martin of New York, who married the fourth Earl of Craven in 1893, brought wonderful jewels as part of her dowry: they included the ruby and diamond tiara and bracelets from the parure made for the Duchesse d'Angoulême — only surviving child of Louis XVI and Queen Marie Antoinette — sold with the French crown jewels in 1887. It was sold by Sotheby's on 30 November 1961.

South African Diamonds

The Victorian passion for display coincided with the discovery of vast diamond deposits in South Africa which made it possible for every woman of means to shine like a constellation. The first authenticated Cape diamond, the 10.73 carat Eureka, found by a bushman digging for roots in December 1866 and given to the children of the local farmer to play with, was bought by the third Marquess of Bute — then the richest man in the world — who had it set in a bangle for his wife Gwendalen. Lent to the Paris Exhibition of 1889, the blue velvet box was stamped in gold THE CENTRE STONE OF THIS BRACELET IS THE EUREKA DIAMOND BEING THE FIRST DIS-COVERED IN SOUTH AFRICA. THE REMAIN-ING STONES ARE ALL SOUTH AFRICAN MOSTLY FROM THE MINES OF KIMBERLEY, and the bangle was inscribed THE EUREKA DIA-MOND FIRST FOUND IN SOUTH AFRICA. Marchioness Gwendalen left it to her son Lord Colum Crichton Stuart, who sold it at Christie's on 17 April 1946. This historic stone, whose discovery led to the industrialisation of South Africa and the pre-eminence of the diamond in jewellery, was presented in 1967 to the Kimberley Mine Museum by De Beers.

The Great Hostesses

Stafford House, the London home of Harriet Duchess of Sutherland, was like a renaissance palace. Lady Eastlake, wife of the Director of the National Gallery, was overwhelmed by the splendour: 'No picture by Paul Veronese of a marriage feast can exceed in gorgeousness what was presented to our eyes'. Duchess Harriet always looked like an empress and at Queen Victoria's wedding, with three rows of diamonds standing up on her head, she shone like the Koh-in-Noor. At Woburn Abbey successive Duchesses wore the Bedford heirlooms with great distinction: a heavy eight-row pearl necklace, pear pearl earrings with diamond cluster tops, pearl stomacher, two parures — one of diamonds, the other of amethysts nestling in diamond vine leaves — and a royal gift, a bracelet with Queen Victoria's miniature. The portrait of Duchess Anna Maria, wife of the seventh Duke,

painted in her coronation robes by John Catterson Smith in 1838, is still in the picturesque style of the Romantic period. That of her successor Duchess Elizabeth, wife of the ninth Duke, by Richard Buckner epitomises the grandeur of the Victorian era (Plate 179).

This was the age of the political hostess and, of all the wives of successful statesmen, none lived in greater style than Hannah Rothschild who married Archibald Primrose fifth Earl of Rosebery in 1878 but died in 1890 leaving three children, who eventually shared her jewellery. Lady Eastlake wrote an account of her visit to Mentmore, the Buckinghamshire home of Hannah's parents, in 1872:

it was like fairyland when I entered the great palace and got at once into the grand hall 40' x 50' and about 100' high hung with tapestry, floored with parquet covered with Persian carpets: an open arcade runs round and looks down through arches into the hall which is filled with gorgeous masses of flowers and every sumptuous object that wealth can command. From this great centre hall branch off lobbies floored with white marble, then three splendid drawing rooms, two libraries, a billiard room with every place almost crammed with precious articles in enamel, bronze, gold, silver, amber, jewels etc...I don't believe the Medici were so lodged at the height of their glory.

As the heiress of so much splendour Countess Hannah's jewels were much commented on. At a reception given by the American writer Oliver Wendell Holmes in 1886, according to the *Illustrated London News*, 'her diamonds shone like the midday sun and her grey satin dress opening at the left side over a panel of ruby and pink striped satin was finished at the bust with a berthe of pink velvet. There was a large spray and aigrette of brilliants in her hair, a collet necklace with a big pendant headed by a Countess's coronet in diamonds, a chatelaine with three large stones in the chain, on the watch and in the coronet above'. Three years later during the state visit of the Shah of Persia her jewels made a wonderful display at the opera: 'On her head was a large ornament like a rose starting from which and passing round the hair was a chain of diamonds that had depending from it festoons and rose-buds all of the same flashing stones: while the white ribbed silk bodice was ornamented all round the berthe with sapphires of unusual size set with diamonds in brooches.' Again, the Ladies Columnist of the *Illustrated London News* described the magnificent scene:

Never was there a more brilliant sight than was presented at the State visit to the opera. The house was crammed with the cream of London society, making such a show of fine gowns and superb diamonds as can hardly be imagined. I have seen many fine sights, but never anything to compare with that presented when the whole company stood in stalls and boxes while the national anthem and the Persian national air were played. White was worn by so many women that it might have been a uniform, but a few dresses in more vivid hues broke the monotony; while the men were nearly all in brilliant-coloured uniforms, or in levée dress with its sheen of velvet and sparkling buttons. Every chair had a large white satin programme pinned against its scarlet back, and on the fronts of all the boxes, to the very top of the house, were laid beautiful bouquets tied up with wide streamers of pale-blue, yellow, or pink ribbon. Behind these the brilliant light of the great chandelier glittered on satin and silk, threw up the colours of scarlet or blue and gold-laced uniforms, and flashed back in a million sparkles from as many superb diamonds, sapphires, and emeralds decking stately heads, white bosoms, and rounded arms.

The first Earl of Dudley was proud of the elegant figure and classical profile of his wife Georgina, and enjoyed spending the revenues from his coal mines on jewels for her (Plate 146). The wonderful jewel casket she received as a bride inevitably invited gossip because she was so much younger than he. Lady Stanley of Alderney, having seen two of his presents – a lovely rope of pearls and a ruby and diamond coronet – declared that Georgina 'would be a happy woman if they were sufficient, but they still say she wanted to cry off even the last day, and people in the crowd round the church called out Shame'. Countess Georgina's jewels won an international reputation: at the Paris Exhibition of 1868 great crowds came to look at her glorious diadem and diamond and emerald parure at the stand of Hunt and Roskell. The Dudley diamond tiara with the 'Star of South Africa' at its centre and necklace with pendants 'as big as pigeon's eggs' were shown by C.F. Hancock at the Vienna Exhibition of 1873 on a stand designed as a medieval jeweller's shop. The Earl and Countess rented a palace

for part of the Exhibition and she became a celebrity. People turned to stare at her whenever she drove out in her barouche escorted by footmen in powdered hair and the smart Dudley liveries. Widowed in 1885, the *Illustrated London News* reported her looking beautiful at the Queen's Drawing Room of 1889, 'in petticoat and bodice of white satin embroidered in silver, a big Empire sash outlining her slender graceful waist edged with a silver fringe, her shoulders fastened with sapphires, the same stones in her stomacher, a velvet sapphire-blue train and sapphire and diamond jewels'.

The Dudley collection did not remain intact: their son, the second Earl, sold 'The Casket of Magnificent Jewels collected during a long course of years by a deceased nobleman acknowledged to have been one of the greatest Connoisseurs of his day', at Christie's on 4 July 1902. The quality was superb. She often wore a string of perfectly white and round pearls on their own with no other jewels, not even on her head. The exquisitely rosy pink Dudley pearl (Plate 146) weighing 209 grains fetched a record £13,500 at the time: this is now in a famous New York collection. Only part of the Dudley jewels were disposed of at this sale; the rest remained in the family who both altered them and bought additions. The flawless quality 47.69-carat Star of South Africa, first exhibited in the tiara by Hancock in Vienna in 1873, was disposed of privately sometime later. Most recently it appeared in a sale at Geneva at Christie's on 2 May 1974, hanging from a small diamond chain: the price was £225,000.

Victorian Taste and Design

Since artistry was of less consequence than the value of diamonds and coloured stones the Victorian jeweller played safe. Most designs – scrolls, ribbons, feathers, flowers, leaves, stars and crescents – are uninspired, and many are no more than monotonous rows of stones graduated in size. Those made of less expensive materials to wear with daytime clothes showed more

Plate 146. Georgina, wife of the first Earl of Dudley. She wears a diamond cluster choker and the famous Dudley pink pearl in its diamond mount hangs from her pearl necklace.

originality and demonstrated a passion for the past just as keen as that of the Romantic period. Mrs Haweis, the influential journalist and author of *The Art of Beauty*, was an enthusiast: staying in a house party at Broadlands, Hampshire home of Lord and Lady Mount Temple, in 1875 she admired the Celtic necklace worn by the rich and clever Lady Ashburton, 'of pure gold which I would rather have than diamonds'.

Another woman who preferred history to mere glitter was a member of the family of the Duke of Atholl who wore a demi-parure as a souvenir of a visit to Greece which is still at Blair Castle, labelled ATHENS MAY 1866. The brooch and earrings are made of ancient silver coins set in gold fret borders. A much wider choice of archaeological-style jewellery was available from Rome where the great master Alessandro Castellani who had won world fame at the international exhibitions lived and worked. His shop at the Piazza di Fontani di Trevi was like a museum, and his designs were based on the ancient Etruscan and Roman jewels in his own collection. For the wedding of Emily Bootle-Wilbraham and the future twenty-sixth Earl of Crawford and Balcarres in 1869 he made a pair of earrings, and a tiara and necklace of golden myrtle leaves with pearl berries — symbolic of wedded love: they are now in the Victoria and Albert Museum. Copies of jewels worn by her Viking ancestors given to the Princess of Wales as wedding presents in 1863 aroused such interest that under her patronage the Copenhagen firm of A. Borgen opened a branch in London. The Countess of Rosebery was a client and bought a silver suite of high collar — five rows deep, each row decorated with filigree — bracelets, brooch and earrings (Plate 147). The original, from Alleberg, Vastergötland, of sixth-century date, is in the Stockholm Museum: the Rosebery copy is still in the family.

Also of sixth-century design is the round-headed Sutherland cross with gold Celtic scrolls set with pearls from rivers on the estate (Plate 148). It is a copy of the crosses marking graves beside the monastic ruins on the island of Iona. Since these monuments of the days when Iona was the centre of Celtic christianity have a special significance for the people of Scotland the present owner, the Countess of Suther-

Plate 147. Silver Viking-style suite copied by A. Borgen of Copenhagen and London from the sixth-century original in the Museum of Stockholm, and worn by the Countess of Rosebery.

Plate 148. The Sutherland gold cross of Celtic design set with pearls fished on the estate.

land, has lent it to the Bishop of Moray, Ross and Caithness.

No Victorian ancestral jewellery is imbued with a stronger historical spirit than the Devonshire parure, commissioned from C.F. Hancock by the sixth Duke of Devonshire for Countess Granville, the wife of his nephew, to wear to the coronation of the Tsar Alexander II in Moscow in 1856 (Plate 149). Of the seven pieces, four – bandeau, comb, coronet and diadem – are for the head, and there are a stomacher, necklace and bracelet. They are set with eighty-eight cameos and intaglios bought by the connoisseur second Duke early in the eighteenth century. Some of these gems are masterpieces from the court workshops of Rome and Alexandria in the first century B.C., but there are excellent examples of Renaissance engraving

too. Portraits of Tudor and Stuart monarchs – Henry VIII, the infant Edward VI, Mary I, Elizabeth I and Charles I – strike a distinctively English note as do the Renaissance style floral mounts, similar to that framing the negress cameo on the Gresley jewel at Southside House (Plate 7). As an afterthought, C.F. Hancock decided to enrich these settings with three hundred and twenty diamonds which were also supplied by the Duke of Devonshire. Hancock explained in a letter to the architect, Sir Joseph Paxton, the Duke's intermediary: 'I found it necessary in the progress of the work to put diamonds round the cameos in order to light it up otherwise the whole parure would have been heavy and utterly spoilt.' In 1857, accompanied by her husband wearing the Order of the Garter and in full diplomatic dress,

Plate 149. Coloured lithograph of the Devonshire parure: bandeau, comb, diadem, coronet, necklace, stomacher and bracelet set with ancient and Renaissance engraved gems in enamelled gold studded with diamonds.

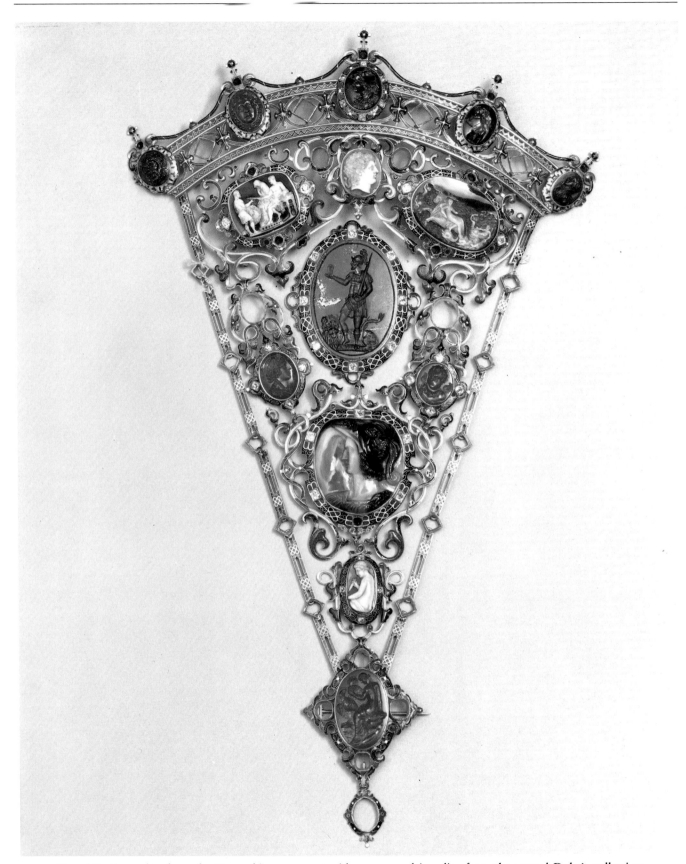

Plate 150. Stomacher from the Devonshire parure set with cameos and intaglios from the second Duke's collection.

Plate 151. Pendant in the neo-Renaissance style representing
Fortune. According to the inscription on the box it was given to
Marchioness Georgina, wife of the third Marquess of Exeter, on
their twenty-fifth wedding anniversary, 17 October 1873, and by
her to Myra, wife of their grandson, in 1905.

Countess Granville in white satin gown, trimmed
with flowers and diamonds, wore the parure again to
a State Ball at Buckingham Palace. It is still at
Chatsworth, kept in a special show-case in the private
apartments.

The Devonshire parure was lent to exhibitions and
set a fashion for neo-Renaissance jewellery, particularly 'Holbein' pendants – usually set with rich red
carbuncles – with borders similar to those designed
by C.F. Hancock. A brightly enamelled gold pendent

allegorical figure – perhaps Fortune – standing on a
globe at Burghley House illustrates the revival of
the sixteenth-century figurative style (Plate 151). It is
in a box inscribed: To GEORGINA SOPHIA
CECIL ON THE 25TH ANNIVERSARY OF HER
WEDDING DAY FROM HER AFFECTIONATE
HUSBAND OCT 17 1873, and then GIVEN BY
HER TO MYRA EXETER MARCH 14 1905 (wife
of the fifth Marquess of Exeter, Marchioness
Georgina's grandson).

The Victorians also revived medieval and Tudor jewels based on monograms, heraldry and coronets. The architect William Burges must have had a Plantagenet princess in mind when he designed a brooch with the arms of Bute for Gwendalen Mary Fitzalan Howard for her marriage with the third Marquess of Bute. It is a Gothic letter G – for Gwendalen – enclosing the two family coats of arms, with three shield pendants hanging below, and surmounted by her marchioness's coronet. The back is inscribed with the date of the wedding, APRIL 16 1872, and the Biblical phrase AMABALIS UT RACHEL SAPIENS UT REBEKAH FIDELIS UT SARAH (Loving as Rachel, wise as Rebecca, faithful as Sarah), the bridegroom's initials repeated twice, and GMAH and GMAB, the bride's initials before and after marriage (Plate 152). The brooch, which was a great success, has been kept in the family.

Similarly noble in character are two other coronet and initial jewels. One is a crowned diamond and rock crystal heart ornamented with a Gothic letter M (Plate 153): a peeress of that name wears it today as a pendant to her rivière. The other is a demi-parure bought by the third Marquess of Exeter for his wife Georgina Sophia from the firm of London and Ryder. The large gold pendant – worn from a supple gold chain – and the matching earrings are set with dark purple amethysts (Plate 154). The coronets surmounting the earrings denote Marchioness Georgina's high rank, while the inscription stamped on the cover of the box proclaims her domestic virtues: TO THE BEST OF WIVES AND MOTHERS FROM HER AFFECTIONATE HUSBAND APRIL 30 1871 GSC (Georgina Sophia Cecil) (Plate 155).

Plate 152. Jewelled Gothic revival brooch in form of the initial G designed by William Burges as a gift for Gwendalen Fitzalan Howard on her marriage to the third Marquess of Bute in 1872.

Plate 153. Diamond and rock crystal heart-shaped locket with crowned family initial M. This hangs as a pendant from a diamond necklace.

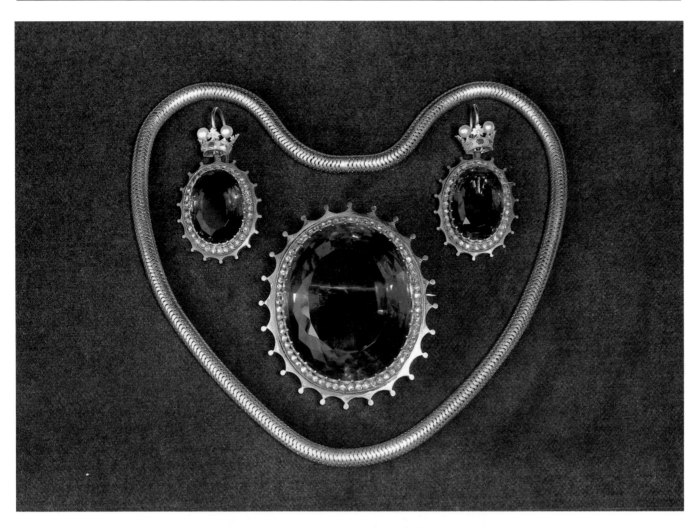

Plate 154 (*above*). The Exeter demi-parure bought from London and Ryder by the third Marquess for his wife Georgina Sophia: the earrings are surmounted by a jewelled marquess's coronet.

Plate 155 (*left*). The original box for the Exeter demi-parure, stamped TO THE BEST OF WIVES AND MOTHERS FROM HER AFFECTIONATE HUSBAND APRIL 30 1871 G.S.C.

Plate 156 The Willoughby owl, paved with diamonds with ruby
and sapphire collar and ducal coronet.

Family emblems were suitable commemorative gifts for the bridesmaids at aristocratic marriages. Those who attended Lady Harriet Godolphin Osborne when she married Mr H.F. Cavendish Bentinck in July 1888 were given brooches with his crest, the Cavendish snake, in brilliants. The bridesmaids at the wedding of the Hon. Arthur Pelham and Miss Evelyn Cust in 1879 wore silver buckles. The Pelhams adopted the buckle as a badge after Sir John Pelham captured King John of France at the Battle of Poitiers in 1356 and bound him with buckled straps. The Ormonde, Stafford and Heneage families – among others – had a distinctive knot as their emblem and these were made into brooches (sold by Christie's on 12 July 1950) and even tiaras (sold by Christie's on 23 February 1949). A diamond necklace of Stafford knots was one of the long list of valuable wedding presents – filling two pages of *The Times* – given to Miss Millicent St Clair Erskine when she married the future fourth Duke of Sutherland, then Marquis of Stafford, in October 1884. Doubtless this has either been remodelled or stolen, as was the fate of most of the Sutherland jewels. The diamond Willoughby owl

(Plate 156), wings stretched out wide, claws gripping a branch with ruby and ducal coronet has, however, descended in the family: the present owner wears it as a stomacher brooch, as did her husband's grandmother. It is one of the great successes of English jewellery, on account of its excellent quality and whimsical character.

Not all heraldic jewels are as luxurious as the Willoughby owl. The tortoiseshell brooch of the Gorges family – a whirlpool with spiral curves outlined by gold headed pins – is extremely effective: it is still kept in the jewel box in which it travelled to Australia and back in the mid-nineteenth century, and is now owned by the great-great-granddaughter of the original owner.

Enamel was also used successfully in Victorian designs: a particularly attractive piece of jewellery still belongs to the present Duke of Portland. It is the badge of the family in bright colours with motto CRAIGNEZ HONTE (Fear shame) worn by his grandmother, Mrs George Augustus Cavendish Bentinck, as a belt buckle (Plate 157).

Plate 157. Armorial belt buckle enamelled with the Portland badge and motto CRAIGNEZ HONTE.

The Scottish nobility and gentry were even more conscious of their history, for each clan had its own distinctive plaid. The shoulder brooches, belt buckles and dirks worn by men with Highland dress of kilt and velvet jacket were often embellished with the owner's crest, as was the brooch which pinned feathers to the bonnet. They were not worn exclusively by men, and at dances women would fasten their plaid scarves at the shoulders with crested brooches. Some were armorial — for example the Breadalbane boar's head, and the Sutherland cat (Plate 235): others, such as the Drummond holly, the Rose briar-rose and the Mackintosh box-wood, were naturalistic. The

fashion for tiaras in the shape of wreaths of heraldic leaves seems to have begun in 1849 when the Duchess of Argyll appeared at the Queen's Birthday Drawing Room crowned with diamond oak leaves, emblem of the Campbells. As a compliment to his son-in-law, Colonel William Gordon Cuming, the eighth Lord Middleton gave his daughter Lettice a tiara of ivy leaves when they married in 1895 (Plate 158). Paved with diamonds, the wreath of twelve leaves and berries looks equally well whether placed on the head or encircling the throat as a necklace. This is still in the family.

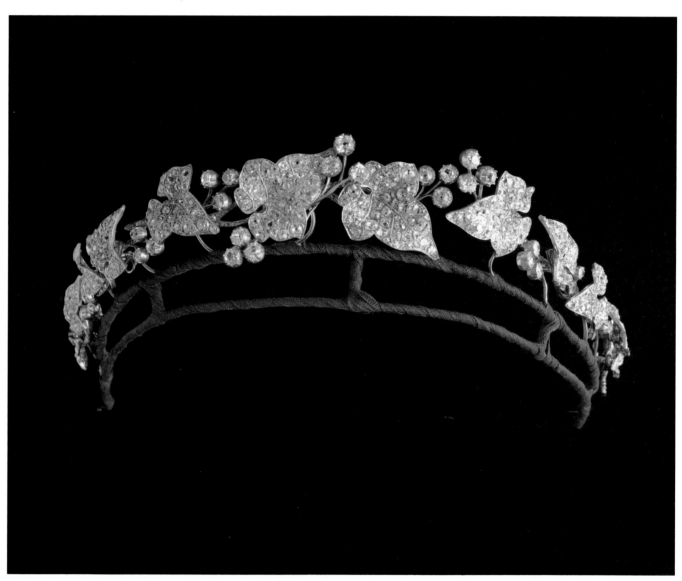

Plate 158. The Gordon ivy-leaf tiara made for Mrs Gordon
Cuming on her marriage in 1895. It can also be worn as a necklace.

Jewels for the Hair

Nowhere did diamonds show to greater effect than high on the head in tiaras (Plates 159 and 160), aigrettes or pins, blazing under the glare of electric light. On grand occasions a tiara was essential. Flowers, plants and leaves — dog roses, lilies and ferns — never went out of fashion. Harriet Duchess of Sutherland for instance was famous for her splendid diamond wreath of mulberry leaves and berries. Alexandra, Princess of Wales promoted the fringe pattern with tall diamond spikes standing up like the rising sun — derived from the *kokoshnik* or Russian peasant headdress. In 1888 she was given one by three hundred and sixty five ladies as a silver wedding present: it is worn by Queen Elizabeth II today. Another favourite design was a circlet of stars which could be dismantled and worn as brooches (Plates 161 and 162).

On less formal but still grand occasions a wide range of jewelled ornaments might be worn in the hair. Stars were always popular and so were crescents, or new moons; these and the many rose, marguerite, swallow, peacock feather, arrow and insect jewels were often worn for the first time fixed to the wedding veil. They were usually new, bought from one of the London or Paris jewellers, but some were heirlooms. At her marriage to Mr Henry Somerset in 1896 Lady Katherine Beauclerk wore a large diamond butterfly pinned to her lace veil. A gift from his mother, Lady Isabella Caroline, heiress of Charles third Earl Somers, it had come down through three generations. Later on, in the 1880s when hair was worn piled high, combs returned to favour, surmounted by jewelled tops which gave importance to coils at the back of the head. On honeymoon in Paris in 1878 the Countess of Rosebery bought a pair — still in the family — from Boucheron in the Palais Royal: one carried her own initial H, the other the family's R; both were surmounted by her coronet (Plate 163).

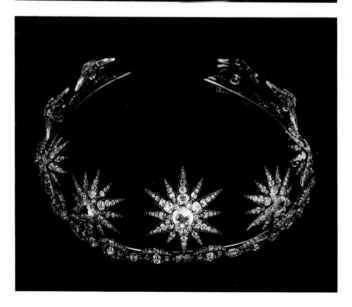

Plate 159 (*top*). Diamond scroll and cluster tiara made for the Countess of Caledon.

Plate 160 (*middle*). The Hambleden diamond and pearl scroll and cluster tiara.

Plate 161 (*bottom*). The Ducie family tiara of stars. They could be removed and worn separately as brooches. The star was the most popular motif in Victorian jewellery.

Plate 162. The Countess of Rosse at the Chelsea Flower Show in 1965 with Victorian star brooches pinned to her coat.

Plate 163 (*below*). Tortoiseshell combs with diamond initials HR surmounted by an earl's coronet. Bought by the Countess of Rosebery from Boucheron in Paris while on honeymoon in 1878.

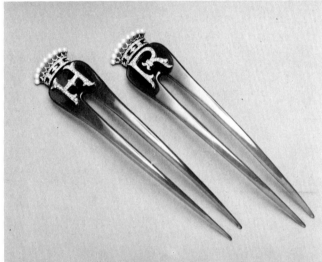

Earrings

Earrings were worn en suite with full or demi-parure ornaments, like the diamond stars in the ears of Miss Violet Brett when she married Mr Dudley Ward in 1876: they were smaller versions of those in the circlet on her head. The tiny ear-tops worn for many years were supplanted by short drops and in the 1890s pear pearls hanging from diamond tops returned to fashion (Plate 164).

Necklaces

Showy necklaces filled the low-cut necklines which for many years were de rigueur with Victorian formal dress (Plate 165). Fortunes were spent on pearls and, being appropriate for day and evening wear, they were almost a uniform for grand ladies. In 1896 the *Illustrated London News* observed that 'the wealthy of this world were wearing long loops of pearls pendent to the waist caught on the bust with a jewelled ornament and the neck encircled with two or three rows of smaller size'. Black pearls were particularly prized, and one of the most famous collections — set in a parure with diamonds — belonged to the Earl of Eglinton. This was sold by Christie's on 22 February 1894.

Diamond necklaces encircled the throat in short chokers or fell down in ropes — some several feet long — massively set in silver. Some sensational necklaces were set with coloured stones in diamond borders, such as the 'magnificent square and oblong emeralds in brilliant scroll pattern frames fringed with pearshaped brilliant drops' in the necklace which Mrs Beckett, a banker's wife, gave her niece on her marriage to Mr Meynell Ingram of Temple Newsam House, Leeds in 1860. This was sold by Christie's on 12 June 1929.

The Princess of Wales introduced high-necked bodices which were permitted on some formal occasions. In the 1890s they were worn with dog-collars of rows of pearls and other precious stones kept in place by diamond bars; some were so deep that they covered the neck almost up to the ears.

Plate 164 (*left*). The Munster demi-parure of pearl and diamond earrings with brooch.

Plate 165 (*opposite*). The St John of Bletso family diamond necklace of wild roses.

Pendants and Crosses

Frances-Anne Marchioness of Londonderry had all her diamonds reset by Garrard's in the 1850s into a splendid parure. The largest and whitest stones inherited from her brother-in-law, the second Marquess, were removed from his sword of honour and mounted in a Latin cross to hang from her rivière (Plate 260). Diamonds also highlighted crosses set with pearls or coloured stones.

Square, lozenge-shaped, oval or round clusters set with important gems or pearls in diamond frames were the conventional choice for pendants. Occasionally an original design is recorded, such as the exotic gold pendant fig in the Pennington-Mellor-Munthe collection at Southside House (Plate 166). It is set with a large cabochon sapphire, inscribed in Arabic which translates, GOD GAVE YOU TO ME: GOD WILL KEEP YOU FOR ME! framed in a double row of brilliants. When Mrs Pennington-Mellor wore this jewel to a reception at the Royal Palace in Athens in 1893, the Queen of Greece, whose aunt was Russian, recognised it immediately, and told her that it was the Romanoff talisman which had been lost by the imperial family some years before.

Brooches

Brooches were essential to Victorian dress. The stomacher which the Marchioness of Londonderry gave her daughter Lady Frances Vane on her marriage to the future Duke of Marlborough in 1843 is an excellent example of impressive but simple Victorian design (Plate 167). It was set with a splendid lozenge-shaped emerald amidst diamonds, hung with an emerald drop and surmounted by a bowknot. It was sold by Sotheby's on 21 January 1981.

Plate 166 (*top*). The Romanoff talisman. A cabochon sapphire fig inscribed in Arabic GOD GAVE YOU TO ME: GOD WILL KEEP YOU FOR ME!

Plate 167 (*right*). Diamond and emerald Sévigné brooch given by the third Marchioness of Londonderry to her daughter Lady Frances Vane on her marriage to the seventh Duke of Marlborough in 1853.

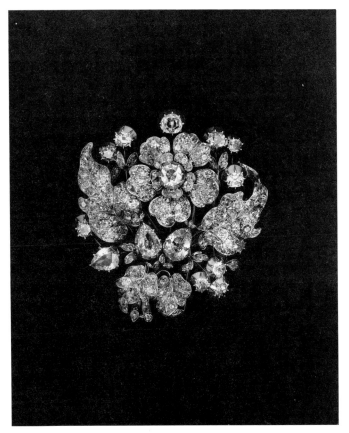

Plate 168. The Sutherland wild rose brooch, set with diamonds.

Plate 169. Set of diamond scroll brooches, heirlooms of the Dukes of Newcastle, representing the conventional and massive Victorian style of formal jewellery.

As might be expected, Lady Dudley's collection boasted several different highly fashionable brooches: a sapphire framed in two rows of diamonds, a turquoise and brilliant oval cluster, a shell entirely paved with brilliants with a large pink pearl in the centre, and bow-knots or sévignés hung with pendants or fringes. These were sold by Christie's on 4 July 1902. Long sprays of flowers — life-sized convolvuli, and waterlilies with yellowish Cape diamonds in the centre, wild roses and leaves (Plate 168), their stalks tied with flowing ribbons — were worn across the bodice from the top of the shoulder down to the opening of the heart-shaped or low square neckline. Not just one, but several jewelled and pearl stars, clusters, butterflies and bugs — chosen at random from the jewel box — might be pinned on the full skirt or ample bodice. Although many were broken up in this century these can still be found in ancestral jewel caskets.

Bracelets

In 1850 the *Illustrated London News* announced that 'Dresses are always with plain body open in front and high at the back with very open and rather short sleeves. This fashion neccessitates the wearing of bracelets and of these there are some of every sort'. Snakes were at the zenith of fashion. They appeared in almost every list of wedding presents: when Caroline Fairfax-Lucy of Charlecote married Major-General Charles Powlett Lane in 1857 her present from the tenants on the estate was a snake bracelet, its coils enamelled blue and the head studded with diamonds. In mid-century, snakes were rivalled in popularity by Garter designs sometimes plain and buckled, sometimes inscribed with the motto from the badge of the Order of the Garter HONI SOIT QUI MAL Y PENSE (Shame be to he who thinks evil of it). A bracelet with this, given in 1853 by

Plate 170. Bracelet inscribed with Garter motto HONY SOIT
QUI MAL Y PENSE and inside WILLIAM SPENCER 6TH
DUKE OF DEVONSHIRE TO LOUISA MARCHIONESS
OF ABERCORN 1853

William sixth Duke of Devonshire to Louisa, Marchioness of Abercorn, was returned to Chatsworth after her death in 1905 (Plate 170).

Many bracelets contained miniatures. Most depict loved ones, sometimes a whole family. The miniatures of the three sons and two daughters of the sixth Baron Monson were painted by the same artist who captured well the strong family likeness shared by all five children, and then set in medallions linked together in a gold bracelet. This was sold by Sotheby's on 8 May 1986.

Memorial Jewellery

The comprehensive collection of memorial rings, lockets, brooches and bracelets at Blair Castle is particularly rich in Victorian pieces. Some are symbolically heart-shaped, all contain hair, identified by inscriptions and crowned monograms, and photographs as well as miniatures. Another fascinating record of the jewels which the mother of a noble family treasured is the 1858 will of Georgiana Countess of Carlisle. Particularly dear was the memory of her eldest daughter Blanche who married the future seventh Duke of Devonshire — her cousin — in 1829 and died in 1840. Blanche's hair was made into a bracelet inscribed HER IMAGE LIVES AMONG THE STONES SHE BLESSES and also placed in a

heart locket inscribed HER LIFE TO WOO US UNTO HEAVEN WAS LENT US HER DEATH TO WEAN US FROM THE WORLD WAS SENT US, bequeathed to Blanche's children, Lady Louisa Egerton and the future eighth Duke of Devonshire, 'hoping that her loved remembrance would never leave their hearts'. Although none of these pieces can be traced today it is clear that they were cherished. A black enamel mourning bracelet for the fifth Duke of Gordon, given by his widow to her sister-in-law, who then bequeathed it to her own daughter, confirms that memorial jewels did indeed pass through several generations. There is a heart-shaped hair locket on the clasp with Gothic letter G and ducal coronet flanked by diamond rays and inside there are inscriptions which record each transfer: GIVEN BY ELIZA DUCHESS OF GORDON TO LOUISA MARCHIONESS CORNWALLIS 28 MAY 1836, and BEQUEATHED TO J. BRAYBROOKE DECEMBER 1850 surmounted by a marchioness's coronet. Hair has been inserted into two spaces under glass in the band. One of Marchioness Louisa's five daughters, Lady Braybrooke — who lived at Audley End in Essex — was to die herself in 1856 having lost two sons in the Crimean War. This monument to Victorian family affection is now owned by Lady Abdy (Plates 171-175).

The Carlisle memorial jewellery is all dispersed

Plates 171-175. THE GORDON MEMORIAL BRACELET. The
heart-shaped black clasp bears the diamond cipher of the fifth
Duke of Gordon, who died in 1836.

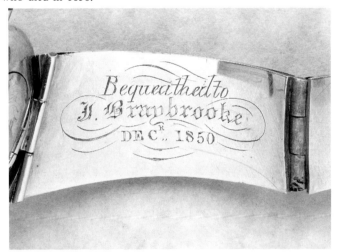

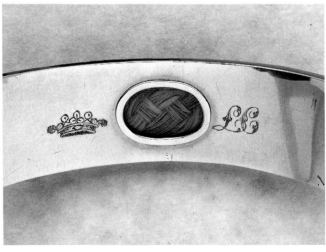

and probably lies somewhere disregarded in boxes of oddments. It is for this reason the survival of the collection at Blair Castle is of such interest, and also the few pieces at Dalmeny Castle, where there are two bracelets of excellent quality, worn by Countess Hannah in memory of her Rothschild relations. Her grandmother, wife of the founder of the British branch of the family, is commemorated by a plain black band inscribed IN MEMORY OF HANNAH DE ROTHSCHILD, set with rose diamonds, with inside Hannah de Rothschild DIED ON THE 5 SEPT 1850 (Plate 176). Hers had been a momentous life: she was beside Nathan Meyer from their marriage in 1806, when he was in Manchester as his father's agent buying manufactured goods, and then watched him make the series of financial coups which led to the move to London. They had a house in Piccadilly — once owned by Thomas Coutts the Regency banker — and another in Gunnersbury. The second bracelet — also black — is fastened by a clasp with a locket outlined in rose diamonds and enclosing a photograph of Baron James, head of the French branch of the Rothschilds: the date of his death, November 15 1868, is inscribed behind.

Photographs and locks of hair of living friends and relations were similarly enshrined. A locket in the Exeter family collection containing photographs of a man and a woman is inscribed AUGUST 3RD 1874: the front is enamelled with a scene of an architect explaining the plans of two buildings to a prince: both are in classical dress. It was worn hanging from a ribbon bowknot loop, on a velvet choker, as described by the *Illustrated London News* in 1868: 'It is the fashion this year for ladies to wear lockets on black velvet ribbon round their necks — the more lockets you can collect and wear the finer you are. Each locket represents an event such as a birthday or anniversary, a bet — any excuse serves as the pretext for giving a locket.' The majority contained locks of hair, both of the living and the dead. They were part of the ritual ornaments worn by brides on their wedding day when they showed their feelings for their future families and their own parents, brothers and sisters, by wearing their hair in jewels. Miss Helen Chaplin, who married the future fifth Earl of Radnor in 1866, placed a lock of the 'dear white hair' of the 'Old Lord' — her future grandfather-in-law — in a diamond and emerald bracelet as a mark of respect for the head of the family she was about to enter.

Plate 176. Plain black memorial bracelet set with rose diamonds and inscribed IN MEMORY OF HANNAH DE ROTHSCHILD.

Gifts from Queen Victoria

Queen Victoria liked to leave bracelets as mementos of her visits to her friends. She much enjoyed her stay at Drummond Castle in 1842: the town of Crieff was illuminated in her honour, Prince Albert went deerstalking and Scottish reels were danced. When it was all over she gave her hostess, Baroness Willoughby De Eresby, a diamond snake bracelet. Most royal bracelets were not so splendid but more personal, with the Queen's miniature on the clasp, gold bands and only a sprinkling of gemstones, if any. There are two, gifts to the Duchesses of Buccleuch (1842) and Atholl (1852), both of whom served as Mistress of the Robes, at Bowhill and at Blair Castle, while a third, at Floors Castle, given to her Lady of the Bedchamber, evokes the sadness of widowhood with its inscription TO THE DUCHESS OF ROXBURGHE FROM HER AFFECTIONATE AND UNHAPPY FRIEND VICTORIA R JUNE 1865. Those privileged to receive these tokens of royal favour wore them with pride and they are depicted in the portraits of Duchess Anna Maria, wife of the seventh Duke of Bedford, and Duchess Elizabeth, wife of the ninth Duke. Duchess Elizabeth's bracelet inscribed TO ELIZABETH DUCHESS OF BEDFORD FROM HER AFFECTIONATE FRIEND VR 1880 is still at Woburn Abbey.

Christmas at Windsor was celebrated in the German style: there was a tree and the Queen gave presents to her guests and to her household. Miss Stanley, a maid of honour, wrote home after Christmas in 1842: 'Lady Douro's present is the usual Lady in Waiting's bracelet with her picture and Miss Hamilton's and mine are of enamel with a little buckle of pearls by way of clasp – it was so nice of the Queen to have given them herself instead of sending them by a dresser.' In 1847 the presents were laid out on a table with a white cloth beside the Christmas fir tree, and Miss Stanley was given a neck chain with a hand in the front holding a ring with a heart-shaped locket. The Duchess of Bedford, who was invited to Windsor for Christmas in 1842, was delighted with her present from the Queen which was also full of sentiment: 'a love of a brooch, a turquoise and pearl dove holding a turquoise heart upon which is a hearts-ease at the back of which is some of her Majesty's hair'.

To her close friend and lady in waiting Frances, daughter of the third Earl of Roden, who married the first Earl of Gainsborough in 1833, Queen Victoria gave a tiara composed of the three national emblems of roses, thistles and shamrocks (sold by Christie's on 10 December 1920) and a gold and lapis lazuli bangle (Christie's, 19 April 1944). When the Countess's daughter, Lady Victoria, married Sir Thomas Buxton in 1862 the Queen's gift was an emerald and diamond bracelet, worn with much pride ever afterwards. Wedding gifts to her numerous god-daughters included lockets with medallic portraits on the cover. These came from the Piccadilly shop of the Neapolitan Carlo Giuliano and were mounted in the neo-Renaissance style at which he excelled. They recall the portrait jewels of Queen Elizabeth I, such as the Heneage locket. Miss Victoria Alexandrina Wellesley received one, framed in opals, when she married Ian Grant Hamilton MP, the future Baron Holmpatrick, in 1877: another was given to Lady Victoria Alexandrina Grey on her marriage to Lewis Dawnay MP in the same year

Plate 177. Portrait medallion of Queen Victoria framed by Carlo Giuliano in neo-Renaissance style.

(Plate 177). This last is now in a private collection.

The most important events in Queen Victoria's life were commemorated by gifts of jewels. As a child, Mrs James Stuart Wortley first met the future Queen at tea during the reign of King William IV, and was also present at the first party given after the accession of 1837: as the only person present on both occasions, the Queen gave her a diamond brooch which as an old lady she always wore on her long trailing black velvet gown. The coronation is recalled by various jewels: a gold bangle with commemorative medal at Floors Castle, a brooch set with a carbuncle above a lock of the Queen's hair inscribed with her cipher and the date 1838 (sold by Christie's on 8 December 1953), and an inscribed ruby and diamond ring given to a trainbearer, also containing hair, which has descended from Lady Mary Talbot to Princess Doria Pamphili in Rome.

Several English families still own the turquoise eagles gripping pearls in their claws which Prince Albert designed for the bridesmaids at their wedding in 1840. The Duchess of Bedford wears hers pinned to a ribbon bow in her portrait by Richard Buckner: both brooch and painting are still at Woburn Abbey (Plates 178 and 179). Another is in the collection of the Marquess of Salisbury at Hatfield, and the Earl of Gainsborough owns a third. His sister, now Lady Maureen Fellowes, wore it pinned to a white dress when she first went to parties as a young girl. A very special gift was made for the royal governess, Lady Lyttleton, when she retired in 1851: 'she feels the parting from all she has lived with for so many years. The royal children have given her a parting gift of a bracelet with their miniatures in medallions all round it: the Duchess of Kent [the children's grandmother] has one the same and they are very pretty. She is much pleased with it.'

Plate 178 (*below*). Turquoise Coburg eagle, worn on the dress of Duchess Elizabeth.

Plate 179 (*right*). Duchess Elizabeth, wife of the ninth Duke of Bedford, by Richard Buckner.

Gifts from Foreign Royalty

According to contemporary memoirs substantial presents were given by foreign royalty. The Emperor Napoleon III and Empress Eugénie of France were particularly generous. They gave Lady Sophie Wellesley, daughter of the British ambassador in Paris, Lord Cowley, a magnificent bracelet when she married Viscount Royston in 1863, and the Marchioness of Ely – lady in waiting to Queen Victoria – was 'quite overwhelmed with lovely bracelets and lockets from the Empress and quite devoted to her'. In 1890 the Dowager Marchioness bequeathed the turquoise and diamond bracelets received at Fontainebleau and the ruby and diamond bracelet from the King of Italy, with her diamond tiara and ornaments, to 'be held on the trusts made by my late son the Marquis of Ely'. Queen Margherita of Italy sent Alberta Victoria, daughter of Sir Augustus Paget, for many years ambassador in Rome, a diamond and sapphire anchor on her marriage to Lord Windsor in 1883. Moved by the assassination of the Earl of Mayo, Viceroy of India, in 1872, the Rajah of Kuppoorthala ordered a symbolic pearl and diamond necklace for his widow from Hunt & Roskell. It was fringed with festoons enclosing stars and lotus buds, emblems of the Order of the Star of India of which the Earl held the Grand Cross. The pendant in the centre, surmounted by an earl's coronet, was inscribed with his initial M in diamonds: below it hung the Rajah's monogram and a large pearl. Another political murder is recalled by a necklace given by Queen Natalie of Servia to Hilda Pennington-Mellor. It is made from the carved emerald scarabs acquired in Egypt by Queen Natalie's grandfather, who had them mounted in Paris as a present for his daughter, Princess Pulcheria, wife of the Austro-Hungarian Prince Sturdza. After her divorce from King Milan of Servia Queen Natalie lived in France. At Biarritz she owned the Villa Sachino, named after her young son Sacha, proclaimed King Alexander of Servia at the age of seven. The Pennington-Mellors were neighbours, and Hilda received a proposal of marriage from the seventeen-year-old King Alexander. After she refused him he married his mother's lady in waiting, Draga Mashin, who was brutally as-

sassinated with him at the Palace of Belgrade in 1903. In memory of the dead king's affection, the bereaved Queen Mother gave Hilda his diamond and cabochon sapphire ring and the scarab necklace which is now in the Pennington-Mellor-Munthe collection at Southside House.

The Marlborough House Set

Queen Victoria abdicated from court life after Prince Albert's death in 1861 and after their marriage in 1862 the Prince and Princess of Wales assumed many of her social duties. They were also the centre of a circle of friends named after their London home, Marlborough House, and linked by a fondness for racing, hunting, cards and parties. In 1875 Marlborough House was the setting for a fantastic costume ball, made brilliant by many family jewels. The Duchess of Wellington wore superb diamonds, and the Duke came dressed as the minister of King Philip IV of Spain, Count Olivares, wearing the collar and badge of the Golden Fleece, as his father had done at Queen Victoria's costume ball of 1845. As Queen Henrietta Maria, the Countess of Hardwicke in black velvet, her black hat looped up with feathers, and the Duchess of Sutherland in white satin hung with ropes of pearls looked as if they had stepped out of the frames of Van Dyck portraits. The next great occasion was the ball at Warwick Castle given by a leading member of the Marlborough House set, the Countess of Warwick, in 1895. The theme was Versailles before the Revolution, and the *Illustrated London News* described Countess Daisy, the hostess, who impersonated Queen Marie Antoinette in:

'paniered' skirt and peaked bodice of Louis brocade, the ground pearl-grey lightly shot with pink, and the floral design in pink, green and gold. A white lace pèlerine finished off the *décolletage* and a long train of blue velvet embroidered with fleurs-de-lis in gold was worn from the shoulders. The high puffed head-dressing was powdered and surmounted with two white and one pink waving ostrich-feathers and a stiff aigrette of blue fixed with diamonds and sapphires and a bandeau of diamonds. A great number of diamonds were pinned to the fichu and stomacher and it is not surprising that the lovely lady who is signalising her accession to the peerage by both social and benevolent activity was on this occasion a perfect vision of splendour. Not less striking appears to have been the appearance of her half-sister, the Duchess of Sutherland, whose dress was of white satin embroidered with gold in an embossed fashion with large birds flying, while her train was of red velvet enriched with gold fleurs-de-lis and bordered with ermine and the Sutherland jewels — rubies, diamonds and sapphires — were worn in profusion.

Although the London setting could not compare with the historic atmosphere of Warwick Castle, the Devonshire House costume ball and dinner party in 1897 (Plates 180-185) was an even greater sensation. Not to be invited was social disaster. The Marlborough House set were there in full force, and put on their disguises with the enthusiasm of children. The hostess, the formidable Duchess Louise, was arrayed in Eastern splendour as Zenobia, the legendary Queen of Palmyra, and her husband the Duke of Devonshire wore black velvet with heavy gold chain as the Hapsburg Emperor Charles V. The costumes and spectacular jewels — some borrowed, but most hereditary — made this evening of pageantry the crowning glory of the celebrations for Queen Victoria's diamond jubilee.

Plate 180. The Duchess of Portland dressed as the Duchess of Savoy.

Plate 181. The Duchess of Roxburghe dressed as Bess of Hardwick.

Plate 182 (*above*). The Marchioness of Tweeddale as the Empress Josephine.

Plate 183 (*opposite, above*). Kathleen Duchess of Newcastle, as Princess Dashkov, with choker and stomacher.

Plate 184 (*right*). The Newcastle bowknot stomacher brooch.

Plate 185 (*far right*). The Newcastle diamond and pearl choker.

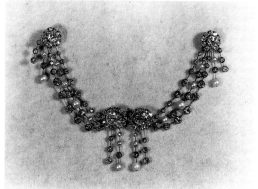

Six
THE EDWARDIANS AND AFTER

A shrewd observer of Edwardian London, the Duchesse de Clermont-Tonnère, decided that the British nobility took their opulent way of life too much for granted: their rank, wealth and privileges, she said, seemed as natural to them as the green leaves on the trees. In Paris there were no more than ten houses where entertaining took place on a grand scale, yet in London she could name at least fifty. She noticed too, that unless desperately ill, nobody missed out on the 'season', a round of racing, balls, dinners, opera, charitable functions and exhibition openings which kept the aristocracy busy from the ritual morning ride in Hyde Park till the last dance in the small hours next day. To her amazement, even the old ladies, who in France were happy to stay at home, continued to go out, dressed up in wigs, and as she put it, 'covered in as many jewels as a medieval shrine'.

Society remained centred on an exclusive group of aristocratic families — impenetrable to outsiders unless they be heiresses to great fortunes — to whom all the great hostesses of the day belonged. Their favourite painter was the American John Singer Sargent whose canvases convey their stately looks and sense of hospitality. They perfected the art of receiving hundreds of guests with the right words of recognition, never forgetting a name or a family history and according each a special greeting. In this league was Millicent, wife of the fourth Duke of Sutherland, who was an

unforgettable sight as she stood beside the statue of a Muse welcoming visitors on the first landing of the wide staircase at Stafford House. Then there was Theresa, married to the sixth Marquess of London-derry who entertained in the grand tradition of his great-grandmother Marchioness Frances Anne, wife of the third Marquess. She was the inspiration for the character of Lady Roehampton in Victoria Sackville West's novel *The Edwardians*. The redoubtable Duchess Louise, hostess of the famous costume ball in 1897 and queen of the racing set, reigned at Devonshire House in Piccadilly. Her appearance was as superb as the lavish setting of the party she gave there in July 1906 which was enthusiastically described in the *Illustrated London News*:

A huge marquee was put up in the garden for supper and a temporary verandah all round one side of the house for sitting out. This was hung with Chinese embroideries and decorated with masses of beautiful flowers. The floral display all over the mansion was exquisite. There were pink and mauve blooms in the ballroom, chiefly in graceful festoons of hydrangeas and geraniums, and single roses — each an exhibition specimen — placed in glass vases on mantlepieces and elsewhere, while the supper room was exclusively decorated with roses. There were crimson ramblers clambering up the stems of growing palms that centred the large tables: other roses were profusely placed in low receptacles of silver and Venetian glass.

Two days later the Duke and Duchess were hosts at

Plate 186. Portrait of Rachel, wife of the second Earl of Dudley,
with her son William Humble Eric, painted by J.J. Shannon.

another party – just as grand – in honour of the King's birthday. They received with old-world magnificence at Chatsworth where guests were welcomed with torches borne by retainers lining the long avenue up to the illuminated house and the Russian Emperor's great fountain, and entertained with dancing, fireworks and amateur theatricals.

King Edward VII sometimes gave the impression that he believed the social fabric would fall asunder unless the protocol governing the wearing of dress, jewellery and decorations was strictly observed. Nowhere was this more important than at court functions, which were particularly brilliant during his reign. Queen Victoria had held her Drawing Rooms in the Throne Room in the afternoon, when few women looked their best in low dresses, feathers and diamonds. When King Edward instituted evening Presentation Courts the scene was transformed: the fifth Earl of Onslow, who was in the embassy in St Petersburg in 1904, said that even the Russian imperial court could not compare with Buckingham Palace. The vice-regal courts of Ireland and India were replicas of St James's in London, and the wives of the Viceroys were dressed and bejewelled like queens (Plate 187). When the Earl of Dudley was appointed to Dublin in 1902, Sir Almeric Fitzroy commented: 'the magnificent of his outlay surpasses all precedent. He is prepared to spend £30,000 a year in excess of his salary and is prepared to be as ubiquitous in Ireland as Lord Curzon has proved in India.' Although some of the Dudley heirlooms had been sold, by Christie's on 4 July 1902, the family still owned an immensely important collection. And they returned from Ireland the richer by at least one piece, the emerald and diamond shamrock brooch for good luck which is still in the family (Plate 206).

That same year there was a tremendous display of jewellery at the Durbar held in Delhi for the coronation of Edward VII, because, as the *Illustrated London News* explained, 'it is felt that it would not be suitable for women of the ruling caste to compare too unfavourably with the native Princes'. The photograph of the Vicereine, the Viscountess Curzon, in the peacock feather dress from Worth of Paris and the jewels which she wore to the Durbar ball, epitomises the elegance and graciousness which

distinguished Edwardian state and ceremony (Plate 187). Lady Curzon's life was short, for she died in 1906, but forty years later the Countess of Asquith still remembered the impression she made on London society.

No smart Edwardian woman would wish to be seen at any time of the day without a string of pearls, a few good brooches, bangles, rings and earrings. At night, in full dress, rivers of stones were worn on the head, round the throat, in wide bands at the waist and hung from the berthe in a fringe trimming the low neckline. This was the style Consuelo Vanderbilt, who married the ninth Duke of Marlborough in 1895, made her own and a description in Lady Monkswell's journals of the slender young American duchess could fit no other: 'a splendid dress of turquoise blue velvet, a little openworked diamond crown perched as they do now on the top of her head, strings of pearls round her neck, a band of diamonds at least three inches wide at her waist'. In 1905 she appeared at a musical soirée at the Austrian embassy in a 'coronet, high crown-shaped, rising at intervals all round in a series of peaks, the tip stone on each peak being an exceptionally large and fine brilliant. She wore a dog-collar of many rows of pearls with diamond slides completely enclosing her throat and many ropes of great pearls besides falling down the bodice'. Her famous triple row of pearls, said to have been worn by Catherine II of Russia and by the Empress Eugénie of France, is worn today by the present Duchess of Marlborough.

Edwardian Taste and Design

Edwardian opulence was kept within the bounds of good taste by new developments in jewellery design and technique. Following the lead of Cartier and Boucheron, who established London branches early in the reign of Edward VII, the leading British jewellers – Garrard, Hennell and Collingwood –

Plate 187 (*right*). The Viscountess Curzon, Vicereine of India, in peacock dress from Worth of Paris at the Delhi Durbar in 1902. The English ladies were requested to wear much jewellery so as not to be outshone by the Indian princes.

substituted light, strong and flexible platinum for massive gold and silver settings. Garlands of stylised flowers and leaves, trellis and lattice-work, and ribbon knots in the Louis XVI style, took the place of the heavy scrolls and monotonous rows of valuable stones which had satisfied Victorian taste. The soft lilac, hydrangea blue and black-and-white gowns made for the Edwardian hourglass figure with its trim waist and full bosom looked well with the monochrome pearls and diamonds which were preferred to bright coloured stones.

Although the Art Nouveau style also represents a reaction to the unimaginative designs of the last decades of the nineteenth century it did not appeal to fashionable English women, so it is not surprising that so few pieces remain in ancestral collections. Even an exhibition of the jewels of René Lalique held at Thomas Agnew's Bond Street picture galleries in 1905 failed to convert them. His exquisitely wrought moths, dragonflies, sweet peas, lilies of the valley and svelte female nudes created from unusual materials such as horn, brightly enamelled and merely high-lighted with diamonds, were bought by very few, and went to provincial Kidderminster and Exmouth, rather than Belgrave Square and Mayfair. While the women with artistic tastes who appreciated Lalique's designs could not afford his high prices, those with money preferred conventional jewels which were not only expensive but looked it. The Countess of Mexborough did own a Lalique fern leaf tiara and Sir Walter Palmer, a politician, acquired a collection for his wife but these were exceptions, disposed of very quickly, for Christie's auctioned the tiara on 11 February 1902, and the Palmer pieces only a few months later, on 20 June.

Tiaras and Aigrettes

As symbols of marital status and rank, tiaras had a special place in society. They were obligatory for many events and even at dinner if royalty was ex-pected. Just before his accession as King, the Prince and Princess of Wales dined in a private house where he reprimanded the Duchess of Marlborough for wear-ing a diamond crescent in her hair, not a tiara, as the Princess had taken the trouble to do. Duchess

Consuelo excused herself on the grounds that she had been busy with charitable work all day and had arrived home too late to get her most valuable jewels from the bank in time for dinner.

Permission was given for tiaras to be worn at the coronation of 1902, an innovation which the courtier Sir Almeric Fitzroy deplored:

The revolt of the Peeresses against wearing no diamonds has ended in tiaras being conceded which, with coronets, will produce as dubious an effect as a man's attempt to wear two hats, besides making it improbable that many will be able to place their coronets on their heads. How-ever, the general sentiment of the sex being in favour of diamonds regardless of tradition and purpose, the dignified uniformity of immemorial practice has been sacrificed to a heedless passion for indiscriminate ornament.

Plate 188 (*above*). Winifred, wife of the sixth Duke of Portland, in her coronation robes. She was Mistress of the Robes to Queen Alexandra.

Plate 189 (*right*). Kathleen, wife of the fourth Duke of Wellington, resplendent in the family lace and diamonds, photographed in 1906.

This departure from tradition, which occurred again at the state opening of Parliament that year when coronets were replaced by tiaras, may explain the flood of commissions which the London jewellers enjoyed at that time. The Duchesses of Beaufort and Norfolk (Plate 190), the Marchioness of Cholmondeley and Lady Desborough were among those who acquired new tiaras, and they lent them to an exhibition held by Cartier at the time of George V's coronation in 1911. The designs — sun rays (Plate 191), ribbons, tassels, swags (Plate 193), wreaths of fern, oak and laurel (Plates 194, 195 and 196) — were mounted in platinum which could support a mass of stones whose weight would have been intolerably heavy if set in gold or silver. Other styles are recorded in the day books of the firm of Hennell: the Russian fringe tiara of Baroness Willoughby De Eresby, the strawberry leaves of Lady Leconfield, the stars of the Marchioness of Bath and, specially commissioned by Sir William Stirling Maxwell in 1901, a lattice work design derived from Celtic miniatures in the Book of Kells, reflecting the influence of Art Nouveau.

Persian miniatures were the inspiration for the exotic diamond aigrette which the Earl of Derby bought for his wife Lady Alice in 1913. The narrow circlet was worn low on the brow — a new fashion for the new century — and the stylised tuft of plumes in the centre was backed by waving osprey feathers. Reminiscent of the oriental fashions of the couturier Paul Poiret, who made the aigrette his own symbol, it is illustrated by Hans Nadelhoffer in his book, *Cartier*, published in 1984. The late Victorian favourites — Mercury wings, lacy bowknots, insects and birds — were not forgotten, but brought up to date in platinum settings which gave a much finer, flatter silhouette.

Plate 190. The Fitzalan Howard diamond oak leaf tiara exhibited by the Duchess of Norfolk at Cartier, Bond Street, in 1911.

Plate 191. Diamond sunray tiara made by Cartier for Mrs
Walter Burns, mother of the Viscountess Harcourt.

Plate 192. The Feversham fringe tiara. The sunray style is derived
from the Russian *kokoshnik* headdress.

139

Plate 193. Diamond tiara with festoons and pear pearls, designed
to be worn high on the head like a crown.

Plate 194. Diamond laurel wreath tiara. This belonged to Margherita Lady Howard de Walden
who wore it when presiding over the annual Queen Charlotte's Ball.

Plate 195. Diamond garland tiara in the eighteenth-century style
revived in the Edwardian period.

Plate 196. Diamond garland and trellis style tiara, another variant
of the Louis XVI style fashionable in the years before World War I.

Earrings

According to the *Illustrated London News*, by 1904 long earrings were at last in fashion again, and when in full dress with a tiara, 'ladies who have them are wearing the very long and large earrings of fine old brilliants which have descended to them from their grandmothers'. New designs of long jewelled chains and tassels were made in platinum.

Necklaces

Several necklaces could be worn with the deep decolletés of Edwardian dress. The Hennell day books record the immense sums spent on pearls, the constant endeavour to improve the quality of existing necklaces, the frequent restringing. Rare, and more costly than diamonds, pearls hung in long sautoirs (ropes) reaching to the waist and fastened with a diamond or coloured stone clasp. The late eighteenth-century negligée returned to favour; that which Lady Nina Balfour bought from Hennell in 1906 – thirteen rows wide – terminated in ruby and diamond balls. The dog-collar remained in fashion at least until 1914. In Anita Leslie's *Edwardians in Love* (1972) a contemporary remembered that it was part of the Hon Mrs George Keppel's attire when King Edward came for tea: 'a black velvet low-cut dress with a huge black feathered hat. As jewellery she wore a high diamond and pearl dog-collar, pearl earrings and diamond drop brooch'. In 1901 the beautiful Lady de Grey bought a dog-collar with a big bowknot in the centre from Cartier: she wears it high on her bare neck in a photograph taken in 1915 (Plate 197). Some openwork designs as fine as lace (Plate 198) were mounted on black moiré silk or velvet so the pattern stood out: the Greek key dog-collar made by Hennell for Lady Alice Shaw Stewart in 1906 was probably worn in this way.

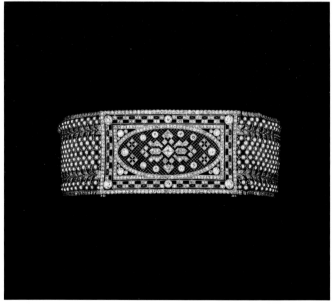

Plate 197 (*top*). Lady de Grey wearing her Cartier dog-collar with diamond bowknot in the centre. The photograph was taken in 1915.

Plate 198 (*right*). Diamond and pearl dog-collar with centre plaque worked like lace: the stones are set in platinum.

The stylised wreaths, ribbons and swags (Plate 193) so successfully used for tiaras made similarly neat and elegant necklaces, for the platinum settings merged with the white light of the diamonds in an apparently single unit. The richest women wore their diamonds — as big as sixpenny pieces — strung together in chains over six feet long. Platinum's unique property, which enabled it to be made up into long jewelled dress chains so fine as to seem almost invisible, meant that diamonds — and also rubies, emeralds and sapphires — seemed to hang as if by magic (Plate 200), and the same principle was adopted for the negligée which often terminated in twin drops or specimen stones. The two diamond and pearl fir cone pendants at the ends of the negligée ordered by the Duke of Westminster from Cartier in 1912 and illustrated by Hans Nadelhoffer in his book stand out all the more in contrast to the slenderness of the chain (Plate 201).

Plate 199. The Fitzwilliam diamond festoon and drop necklace worn by Olive, wife of the eighth Earl.

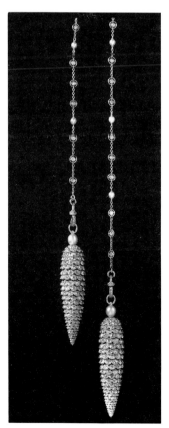

Plate 200 (*far left*). Cartier diamond cascade pendant on platinum chain.

Caption 201 (*left*). Diamond and fir cone pendants on a negligée chain. Bought from Cartier by the Duke of Westminster in 1912.

143

Plate 202. Peridot and diamond pendant worn by the Marchioness
of Exeter. The peridot was the favourite stone of King Edward VII.

Good stones for the centres of necklaces as well as to hang from negligées were always in demand. In December 1914 the Earl of Cadogan instructed Hennell's to find him either a fine sapphire or large diamond for his wife's diamond necklace: they were unsuccessful, and he considered buying a pendant instead. As a compliment to King Edward VII, whose favourite stone they were, there was a fashion for translucent green peridots for necklaces and pendants, usually set round with diamonds: one survives in the collection of the Marquis of Exeter (Plate 202). Lady Eardley, who obviously had a sense of history, was reported by the *Illustrated London News* in 1902 wearing a black and gold dress and a famous pendant which contained the 'stick diamond', so called because it was given by the Empress Maria Theresa to Prince Esterhazy mounted on a stick.

Stomachers, Fringes and Brooches

At her party on the evening of the state opening of Parliament in 1902 the Duchess of Devonshire wore a high diamond crown, pearl necklace with an immense ruby in the centre, ruby brooches and a row of large and splendid brilliants along the lace berthe trimming the top of the black velvet bodice of her Empire-style dress. This Edwardian way of finishing the neckline developed into magnificent fringes of diamonds which cascaded across the shoulders and met at the centre of the bodice in a bow-knot. The Viscountess Hambleden was given a magnificent one on the birth of the future third Viscount in 1903. His widow, the present Dowager Viscountess Hambleden, Lady of the Bedchamber to Queen Elizabeth the Queen Mother, wore it on full dress occasions when the late Queen Mary never failed to notice it (Plate 203). It was sold by Christie's on 14 July 1948.

Large stomacher brooches which covered the bodice with a gleaming mass of jewels appealed to the Edwardian sense of luxurious display. Yet, despite their size and great intrinsic value they were almost always light and graceful compositions of scrolls, garlands (Plate 204) and ribbons (Plate 205). A double bow-knot composed of a ruby ribbon entwined with another of diamonds was ordered by the Viscountess Ridley from Hennell's in 1907: the stones came from two diamond necklaces, a ring, a bracelet and a pendant.

Plate 203. Diamond fringe given to the Viscountess Hambleden
on the birth of her son in 1903.

Plate 204. Sapphire and diamond garland-style stomacher worn
by Olive, wife of the eighth Earl Fitzwilliam.

Plate 205. Diamond bowknot stomacher brooch: an Edwardian
revival of the traditional eighteenth-century design (see Plate 69).

Plate 206. Emerald and diamond shamrock brooch, a gift to the Countess of Dudley while Vicereine of Ireland, 1902–5.

Plate 207. Emerald, diamond and pearl brooch worn by the Countess of Dudley in her portrait (see Plate 186).

Botanical designs remained in fashion. According to the *Illustrated London News*, in 1902 Captain Heneage had his family jewels 'superbly reset for his bride, Miss Helyer, (daughter of Lady Savile) in the form of several collars, necklaces and, most notably, in one large brooch like a rose full blown with buds and leaves in graceful sprays on either side.' Mrs Cavendish Bentinck gave her cousin, Lady Annabel Crewe-Milnes, who married Lord O'Neill that year, a brooch of family interest, set with a large emerald and diamonds from a jewel worn by their ancestress the Duchess of Somerset who was chosen to preside as the Queen of Beauty at the Eglinton Tournament of 1839. This recreation of Plantagenet pageantry – ruined that year by continuous rain – cost the organiser, the romantically minded Earl of Eglinton, £40,000.

Royalty gave brooches as souvenirs of their visits to stately homes. One hostess, the Marchioness of Bath, ensured that her descendants would never forget the illustrious origin of a pearl and diamond brooch given to her and brought it to Hennell's who inscribed it: PRESENTED BY THEIR ROYAL HIGH-NESSES THE PRINCE AND PRINCESS OF WALES JUNE 24 1909 ON THE OCCASION OF THEIR VISIT TO LONGLEAT JUNE 21ST TO 24TH 1909.

Bracelets

Since glitter and scintillation was the rule, several bangles of precious stones were worn on either arm. Every sort – from flexible chains to stiff hoops – was fashionable. Bracelets were conspicuous among the jewels which the Earl of Rosebery gave his children as wedding presents: one set with a huge yellow diamond framed in sapphires to his daughter Lady Sybil Primrose in 1903, and no less than three, all studded with diamonds, to her sister-in-law, Dorothy Grosvenor, who married Lord Dalmeny – the future sixth Earl – in 1909. Lord Rosebery shared between both children jewels worn by their mother, the former Hannah Rothschild who died in 1890 (see chapter 5).

Bracelets, as before, conveyed personal messages. Some were inscribed with christian names, avowals of love and anniversary dates, or were hung with heart lockets and symbols of good luck. Queen Alexandra's lady in waiting the Marquise d'Hautpol, formerly the Hon Julia Stonor, collected charms recording events in court life and wore them from her bracelet which is still in the Camoys family. A diamond monkey charm represents the Portuguese ambassador, the popular Marquis de Soveral, nick-named the 'Blue monkey' on account of his swarthy

Plate 208. Charm bracelet hung with souvenirs of Edwardian
court life, collected by the Marquise d'Hautpol and inherited by
Jeanne, Lady Camoys.

skin, and there are six others: the white rose badge of the Duke of York, crowned with a diamond ribbon; a horse with jockey wearing the racing colours of Edward VII; the coronation medal of 1902 – a personal gift from the King; a mourning pendant from Queen Alexandra inscribed with the date of the King's death, 10 May 1910; a diamond Latin cross; and a diamond ball with two figures of eight, symbolic of good luck, in rubies and sapphires (Plate 208).

Memorial Jewels

The Edwardians continued the custom of remembering the dead by wearing hair enclosed in brooches and lockets. These were usually made of rock crystal with rose-diamond monograms and dates: Hennell's day books record many such commissions, annotated to the effect that any surplus hair must be returned. In mourning for her husband Charles who died in 1915, Theresa Marchioness of Londonderry wore his miniature and a lock of his hair in a diamond locket identified by his crowned cipher.

The Old Order Changes

Just as the Bourbon monarchy and all it represented perished with the Revolution of 1789 so also the Edwardian aristocracy's life of luxury and privilege came to an end after the outbreak of World War I in 1914. There was already evidence of the disintegration of the old order as early as 1906 when the *Illustrated London News* commented, 'our aristocracy have progressively abandoned their old-world state and ceremony'. At the end of July 1914, summing up the past season, a contributor returned to the theme and pointed out 'how comparatively few have been the great entertainments. For one reason or another, several of the best houses in town have not been opened to receive guests at all. The state of the nation in many respects causes anxiety: the vast increase in taxation reduces means, husbands and wives of high rank who cannot agree too often these days allow their personal differences to become public property.'

For some time after the armistice of 1918 social events and valuable jewels did not seem right, and the first sign of a revival of the prewar semi-political, semi-social party was seen at a Londonderry House reception in November 1919 when Edith, wife of the seventh Marquess and the greatest hostess of the interwar years (Plate 209) invited two thousand guests. The Prime Minister, Bonar Law, was there to convey an official atmosphere, and the Marchioness stood at the head of her staircase, smiling and gracious, wearing the same jewels, the same all-round crown as had the wives of the fourth, fifth and sixth Marquesses, all inherited from Marchioness Frances Anne who

had died in 1860. The names of the guests made a familiar roll-call: Derbys, Devonshires, Portlands and Salisburys, though of a different generation and much depleted. It was perhaps significant of the changed political and social mood of the country that the *Illustrated London News* was obliged to defend Marchioness Edith against the left-wing claim that her 'diamonds bought out of profits on black diamonds are the common property of the nation'. Loyally arguing that the Londonderry jewels were in the family before the coal mines, and that the fortune of the Vane-Tempests and the Stewarts had financed their development and given employment, the writer concluded, 'the superb and plenteous jewels are a heritage and one in which Britishers all round take a vicarious pride'.

The Modern Court

King George V decided that court procedures must be adapted to the new postwar circumstances. It was announced that presentations – the ritual initiation of debutantes and brides into society – should take place at four courts held in May and June. At the first court of the 1922 season trains were short – now only eighteen inches long – and plumes low, but there was still an atmosphere of formal magnificence and imposing jewels were worn with the veils, evening dresses and bouquets of flowers. After World War II these functions were succeeded by afternoon presentation parties which in their turn were abolished in 1958 after criticism that the system was being abused by large numbers of *nouveaux riches*. The decision to do away with this prized social credential – for only those who had been presented could attend court balls – made under a Conservative government was a significant step towards the democratisation of Britain, for it disassociated the monarchy from a social élite based on birth.

Plate 209. The Marchioness of Londonderry receiving her guests at an eve-of-Parliament reception at Londonderry House, with Ramsay Macdonald beside her. She wears the tiara of teardrop pearls and the amethyst and diamond chain given to the wife of the third Marquess by the Emperor Alexander I.

Plate 210. Peeresses lined up outside the House of Lords waiting
for their cars after the state opening of Parliament in 1933.

Another occasion which called for a display of jewels was the state opening of Parliament, and in spite of a certain nervousness engendered by the first Labour government of 1924 peeresses continued to wear their best dresses and hereditary jewels. The resplendent example set by Queen Mary was followed by her Mistresses of the Robes: Evelyn, Duchess of Devonshire never failed to dazzle in her high diamond crown and shimmering dress weighed down with decorations (Plate 263) and Eileen Duchess of Sutherland was always elegant in gold satin or brocade glittering with the family diamonds. This pageant of pomp and splendour with fanfares of trumpets continues today and the formal splendour of the bejewelled peeresses makes a striking contrast with the daytime precincts of Westminster, so often muddy and windswept (Plate 210).

King George V's coronation in 1937 encouraged a display in the old tradition which *Vogue* magazine appreciated: 'from the moment we watched those Duchesses, proud as galleons in full sail moving majestically with their tiaras and trains up one of those double staircases, we knew that the social clock had been put back thirty years.' In the same issue there was an eight-page portrait gallery of peeresses photographed by Cecil Beaton in their brocade court dresses under open, miniver-edged robes. He encouraged them to bring all their jewels to his studio and each photograph conveys the glamour of good looks and a lifetime spent in splendid houses rich in treasures and tradition. The Duchess of Buccleuch, sister-in-law of the Duchess of Gloucester, in her tiara, immense diamond collet necklace, huge emeralds and wrists deep with bracelets (Plate 212) bears comparison with the imposing portraits of the Countess of Shrewsbury and the Marchioness of Londonderry at the coronation of William IV (Plates 92 and 125).

Plate 211 (*left*). Portrait drawing by Molly Bishop in 1973 of the Duchess of Buccleuch and Queensberry wearing emerald earrings, necklace and Medusa cameo brooch. Her tiara can also be worn as a belt.

Plate 212 (*right*). The Duchess of Buccleuch and Queensberry in court dress with the Buccleuch jewels, photographed by Cecil Beaton for the coronation issue of Vogue, 1937.

Plate 213. Duchess Deborah, wife of the eleventh Duke of Devonshire, dressed in the robes of Duchess Georgiana, wife of the fifth Duke, for the coronation of 1953.

At the coronation ceremony in Westminster Abbey the diarist Sir Henry 'Chips' Channon was proud of his wife Honor 'splendid in grey with all her sapphires and diamond tiara', and her mother, the Countess of Iveagh, 'magnificent in her glorious diamond rivière which made a circle of blazing light which sparkled as she moved. The north transept was a vitrine of bosoms and jewels and bobbing tiaras'.

Jewels added to the dignity of the coronation of Queen Elizabeth II in 1953 and Cecil Beaton thought the peeresses en bloc were the most ravishing sight, like a bed of auriculated Sweet William with their dark red velvet and foam-white dew spangled with diamonds. The Duchess of Buccleuch and the Countess of Haddington, in huge diamond fenders, were particularly outstanding but the most beautiful of all was young Debo [Duchess of Devonshire] with her hair dressed wide to contain an Edwardian cake-like crown – a Cavendish heirloom. She wore the robes of the eighteenth-century Duchess Georgiana, which are quite different from today's cut with a straight line from shoulder to shoulder (Plate 213).

Plate 214. The Countess of Leicester who attended the coronation as Lady of the Bedchamber to Queen Elizabeth II.

Plate 215. Countess Howe in her coronation robes and spiked tiara.

Plate 216. Lady Howard de Walden photographed by Lenare in her coronation robes and tiara of rising suns and foliage.

The presence of foreign royalty or heads of state on official visits has also consistently been honoured by full dress court ceremonies and entertainments, right up to this day. In 1950, when Monsieur Auriol the President of France and his wife attended a ballet gala at Covent Garden, although the French ladies were most beautifully dressed in *haute couture* they did not wear jewels and as a result it was the bejewelled English peeresses who caught the eye. Two of them wore their old family jewels with particular distinction: the Mistress of the Robes, Helen Duchess of Northumberland was magnificent in tall strawberry leaf crown (Plate 217), long earrings, great diamond rivierè and pearls with diamond clasp, and the Countess of Rosse shone out in her beautiful emerald and diamond tiara with necklace and earrings to match (Plates 218 and 219). Ten years later, when the Countess attended the party held at Buckingham Palace on the eve of the marriage of her son Antony, the future Earl of Snowdon, with Princess Margaret in May 1960, she wore the same superb jewels with a black-and-white organza gown from Victor Stiebel (Plate 220). Every royal wedding since that of Princess Mary to Viscount Lascelles, the future Earl of Harewood, in 1922 has been celebrated by a court ball when those who own fine jewels and tiaras are expected to wear them.

Plate 218. The Rosse diamond and emerald necklace.

Plate 217 (*left*). The Duchess of Northumberland in robes and jewellery painted by Philip de Lászlò, her head crowned with a strawberry leaf tiara. She was Mistress of the Robes to Her Majesty Queen Elizabeth the Queen Mother.

Plate 220. The Countess of Rosse wearing the family jewels (see Plates 218 and 219) to the court ball held at Buckingham Palace before the marriage of her son the Earl of Snowdon with HRH the Princess Margaret in 1960. Her black and white organza dress was made by Victor Stiebel.

Plate 219. The Rosse diamond and emerald tiara with swinging drops.

Jewels for Private Parties

The season did not fully resume until the 1920s and it was some time before the other great family mansions followed the lead of Londonderry House and opened for entertainments. It seemed as if informality was now the rule and when his daughter-in-law wanted to sell her sapphires in 1920 the Viscount Esher agreed and went on to say, 'Jewels are for pleasure – there is no "duty" attached to them. Personally I think those young women will look shabby at big parties without "flashing" jewels, but then "parties" are receding into memories of Edwardian England. You can jazz, I suppose on tea and sandwiches between four and seven.' Lord Esher's pessimism was justified. Not wishing to live in their town houses, let alone hold parties, the owners shut them up or looked for tenants: The Marquess of Lansdowne, for one, let his Berkeley Square home – Lansdowne House, built by Robert Adam – to Gordon Selfridge in 1922. Some families eventually weathered the storm and by 1929, when the Earl and Countess of Dudley gave a ball at Dudley House, it seemed as if the old order had been restored. According to *Vogue*:

Lord Chesterfield was wearing his diamond Garter...as one surveyed the scene with men in pre-Bastille court breeches and the women covered in jewels one felt a whiff of the eighteenth century pass through the heated room. Duchesses were well represented. Her Grace of Sutherland with her original diamond headdress across her hair in bands carried the most ornamental of rainbow ostrich feather fans and was in black like Lady Bessborough and Lady Dalmeny. The jewels were divine. Apart from Her Majesty's diamond tiara the finest collection to my mind was worn by Lady Cholmondeley (in a very short printed black and white frock) who exhibited a diamond and sapphire tiara and five ropes of the most magnificent pearls. She told me that the stones in the tiara originally came from the royal crown of France. Mrs Walter Burns (niece of Pierpont Morgan, the American financier) and the Duchess of Roxburghe came next in my estimation'.

The younger people wore cabochon or carved oriental stones, a fact which the Maharanee of Cooch Behar had pointed out to the *Vogue* correspondent a few nights before. This revival of the fashion started by the English eighteenth-century nabobs was the inspiration of Jacques Cartier, who bought these stones on his regular visits to India.

A reporter at Londonderry House the same year was also impressed by the jewels: 'I liked the early Victorian and grand effect of the flowers and truly amazing jewels on the dress of our hostess. The Duchess of Portland was in white with a diamond bow having a large ruby in the centre, Lady Hambleden wore a diamond key pattern tiara...the smartest was Lady Cholmondeley in blue tulle over net her only ornament being four rows of the Cholmondeley pearls'. By the 1930s, when Margaret Whigham, later Duchess of Argyll, was the reigning debutante the number of houses open for private entertaining had increased and during the season she went to balls and receptions almost every night, where the men wore white tie and tails, the women full evening dress. But this period was brief and one by one Hampden House, Devonshire House, Warwick House, Sunderland House and all the other great houses were sold for redevelopment. The last survivor, Londonderry House, was demolished to make way for a hotel in 1962.

A New Generation, the Old Jewels

According to *Vogue*, the postwar social world 'had become an oyster which lay ready for any adventurer to open with a sword'. American hostesses had arrived: some, like the Countess of Granard and Lady Cunard, had married Englishmen, while the husband of the Viscountess Astor had settled here. The Astors in particular entertained grandly; at a big evening party in 1921 following a dinner in honour of the retiring American ambassador, Mr Davis, and his wife at her house in St James's Square Viscountess Astor stood out in a black dress with diamond necklace and brooches and the historic Sancy diamond – now in the Louvre – flashing out from the centre of her tiara. Mrs James Corrigan, once a typist from Wyoming and now the extremely wealthy widow of a steel magnate, rented No. 16 Grosvenor Street and a guest list from the Hon Mrs George Keppel and gave extravagant parties which became the talk of the town. Her jewels were amazing and she liked to give presents to favourites such as Edith, Marchioness of Londonderry. There is a photograph of an emerald and diamond bracelet which Mrs Corrigan gave her in the album listing the family jewels at Mount Stewart, Irish seat of the Londonderrys (Plate 221).

A new generation of English hostesses had also grown up. The picturesque and cultivated Viscountess Wimborne held candlelit musical evenings at Wimborne House in Arlington Street, and above all there was Edwina Ashley, who married Lord Louis Montbatten in 1922. She had good looks, great taste, a large fortune inherited from her grandfather Sir Ernest Cassel, the Edwardian financier, and through her marriage she was connected with royalty. She entertained well at Brook House in Park Lane and at Broadlands in Hampshire. The antithesis of the Belle Epoque corseted hour-glass beauty, she represented the new emancipated woman with her short hair and slim-skirted, straight silhouette. Her jewels were equally modern and, among the many women in society who patronised contemporary jewellers, her collection was outstanding. The casket of jewels she inherited from her mother and received as a bride formed the basis of a collection – bought from the great houses of Cartier, Boucheron and Lacloche – which illustrated the sequence of styles in fashion from her marriage in 1922 up to the early 1960s. Her mother's garland-style stomachers, aigrettes and dog-collars were sold or broken up, and the stones reset in long tapering earrings which almost reached her shoulders, broad bracelets and necklaces in geometric designs (Plates 222 and 223) which owed nothing to the past but echoed the Cubist art of Picasso and the streamlined architecture of the Bauhaus. Some were entirely set with diamonds in a variety of cuts, others were bright with contrasting colours – amethyts and topazes, acquamarines and cabochon sapphires. The floral brooches and earclips she wears in photographs dating from the 1940s and 1950s represent the reaction from the austerity of the 1920s and 1930s. Various pieces, including an emerald necklace, were made to her husband's design. Her last purchase, a brooch of five quaintly individualised birds perched on a branch, belongs today to her daughter, Countess Mountbatten of Burma, who shares the collection with her sister, Lady Pamela Hicks. As consort to

Plate 221. Diamond and cabochon emerald bracelet: a gift for the Marchioness of Londonderry. The emerald was acquired by Cartier from an Indian princely collection.

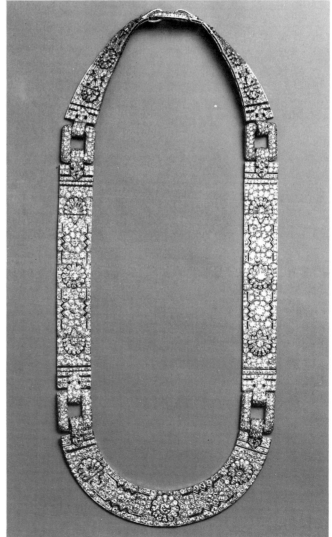

Plate 222. Diamond and platinum Art Deco chain worn by Countess Mountbatten.

Plate 223. Countess Mountbatten dressed for the coronation of 1937 in Art Deco jewellery, photographed by Yevonde.

the last Viceroy of India, who brought British rule to a triumphant conclusion, Countess Mountbatten had worn her jewels in the grand manner (Plate 223). In private life she wore them with wit and no less distinction.

During the interwar years other elegant women — the Marchioness of Dufferin and Ava, Lady Bra-

bourne — wife of the Governor-General of Bengal (Plate 224) — the Countess of Brownlow, and the Baroness Willoughby De Eresby, daughter of the Viscountess Astor — bought equally striking jewels. They are illustrated in the design books of Cartier and of Hennell, where the chief designer was Charles Bruno; the Garrard ledgers also record a large volume

Plate 224. Lord and Lady Brabourne during his term of office as Governor-General of Bengal, 1937–9.

of business. These severely geometric tiaras (Plate 225), necklaces, chains, pendants (Plate 226), bracelets (Plate 227), rings and earrings (Plate 228), pins (Plate 229) and clips for the hat and dress stood out most effectively against plain black dresses and tailored clothes (Plate 230). No jeweller would wish to dis-

close details of transactions made by post World War II clients but the daughters of the previous generation did return to them and bought pieces in quite a different style — made of diamonds in a variety of cuts shooting upwards or swirling round in designs which are full of movement.

Plate 225. Art Deco-style diamond tiara worn by the Countess of Munster.

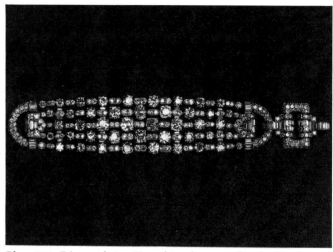

Plate 227. Diamond Art Deco bracelet worn by the Duchess of Sutherland.

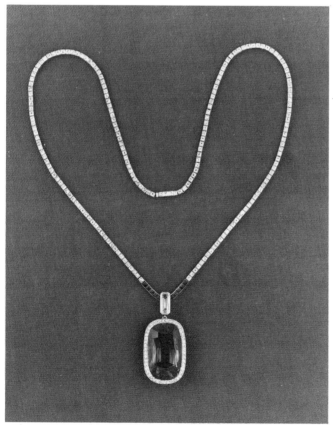

Plate 226. Sapphire pendant on a diamond chain, by Cartier.

Plate 228. A Pair of Art Deco-style diamond earrings: the pendants hang from a chain of baguette-cut stones.

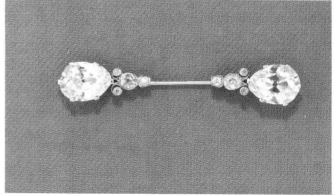

Plate 229. Double-headed diamond sureté pin worn by the Marchioness of Zetland in the 1920s.

Plate 230. Rose, wife of the Earl of Warwick, wearing Art Deco
diamond jewellery, photographed by Paul Tanqueray in 1935.

'Tiaras Will be Worn'

In 1924 the *Illustrated London News* declared that 'Balls for good causes have ousted private entertainment'. Times had indeed changed, but these balls could be the occasion for a display of jewels. The Jewels of the Empire Ball at the Park Lane Hotel in 1930 and the Famous Beauties Ball at the Dorchester were remarkable for the quantity of jewellery worn, and in the 1950s and 1960s bejewelled guests made the Rose Ball at Grosvenor House a glittering occasion. For many years, in the interwar and postwar period, Lady Howard de Walden was president of the Committee for Queen Charlotte's Birthday Ball held on the first Tuesday in May at Grosvenor House. Eleven hundred guests attended and Lady Howard de Walden and the patronesses wore their tiaras (Plates 231, 232 and 233). The ball raised money for Queen Charlotte's Maternity Hospital in the Goldhawk Road, and a card was printed explaining its history:

Queen Charlotte's Birthday Ball was held each year at St James's Palace. She liked to be surrounded by her family and her Maids of Honour and to have her Birthday cake with its lighted candles brought to her to the music of the March from Handel's Judas Maccabeus. She then, herself, cut the cake. She was the first influential lady to take a personal compassionate and practical interest in poor women, ill, in childbirth or homeless. Queen Charlotte's hospital was named after her, and in tribute to her at the ball each year her Birthday party is reenacted with a Birthday Cake and a Guest of Honour who represents Queen Charlotte to whom the Maids of Honour make their obeisance, to the playing of the music the Queen herself chose.

For decades, the Royal Caledonian Ball, where the men wear their clan tartan kilts and velvet jackets, has been one of the most picturesque sights of the London social calendar. The dowagers usually wear black or some rich fabric that sets off their tartans and jewels, the girls and younger women white or pale-coloured gowns. The tartan sashes worn

Plate 231. The Marchioness of Cambridge at a ball in May 1954.

Plate 232. The Duchess of Northumberland at a ball in May 1956.

Plate 233. Countess Cadogan at the Rose Ball in 1957.

over one shoulder are often fastened with family badges worked in diamonds (Plate 234) and other precious stones, one of the most distinctive being the large diamond Sutherland cat (Plate 235) enclosed in a buckled Garter inscribed with the family motto SANS PEUR (Fearless). The *Illustrated London News* described the brilliant scene in 1922:

the Duchess of Atholl with her cream coloured satin and lace gown and tartan sash wore a high tiara of very fine emeralds and diamonds. Lady Glentanar's diamonds were very fine. I was fascinated by a broad band of diamonds worn by the Duchess of Buccleuch across the bodice of her black tulle and jet dress. It was quite two and a half inches broad with a large medallion in the centre and was at once imposing and beautiful for the design was good and the setting superb. The Duchess wore a collet necklace of very large and very fine diamonds and also diamond ornaments in her hair. It was to do honour to the national ball that her Grace of Buccleuch was thus gloriously bedecked. The diamond band must be a girdle in its

ordinary employment and is quite the loveliest I have ever seen and I know three.

A Buccleuch heirloom, this belt was made for the eighteen-inch waist of Duchess Charlotte who married the fifth Duke in 1829: it was worn again as a belt by Duchess Mary in 1937 (Plate 211) and for the coronation in 1953 on her head as a tiara.

The *Illustrated London News* in 1922 discussed the tiara, which for over one hundred years had put the seal of distinction on social events and concluded that 'the tiara is a much derided ornament yet it is a characteristic one of British great ladies and worn by eight out of ten with dignity and imposing effect. Every woman at state functions wears one'. It is thanks to the presence of the monarchy that she can still do so today. Tiaras distinguish official and charitable functions, weddings (Plates 236, 237 and 238) and other great family occasions. Nowadays these are most likely to take place in the country, where

Plate 234. The Duchess of Roxburghe at the Caledonian Ball, 1980, her plaid fastened at the shoulder by a jewelled brooch.

Plate 235. The Sutherland cat in buckled Garter inscribed with motto SANS PEUR, worn with the plaid.

the old tradition of hospitality continues. Just before World War II, looking back over many years of social life, the Countess of Oxford and Asquith observed: 'English society has retired to the country. Gone are most of the great houses of London but the majority of great country houses still go on; and the English country house party keeps the old way of life alive'. This is just as true of the 1980s and it is in these mansions, when celebrating a coming of age, a marriage or special anniversary, in rooms filled with flowers from the garden, gleaming with old plate and hung with historic pictures, that the women guests, afire with ancestral jewels, relive the pageantry of former days (Plate 240).

Plate 236. The Duke and Duchess of Westminster after their wedding in 1978. She wears the Bagration tiara over her veil.

Plate 237. Diamond and spinel tiara made for Princess Katherine Bagration c. 1820, part of a parure bought by the Duke of Westminster for his bride.

Plate 238. The Countess of Dalkeith wears the Buccleuch mayflower tiara at her wedding in 1953: her lace dress is patterned in the same floral motif.

Plate 239 (right). Miss Frances Sweeney with her father before her wedding in 1958 to the Duke of Rutland. She wears his gift, an acquamarine and diamond brooch surmounted by a ducal coronet.

Plate 240 (opposite). Lydia, Duchess of Bedford wearing the family amethysts at a dance at Woburn Abbey in 1956.

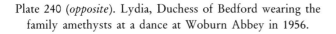

Appendix
WHERE ARE THEY NOW?
DISPERSAL, TRANSFORMATION
AND THEFT

Dispersal, transformation and theft

History has been kind to the British aristocracy. It has been protected from revolution by centuries of stable government and from foreign invasion by our island coastline. Until this century the great estates remained intact thanks to the law of primogeniture whereby only the eldest son inherited and he in his turn passed on not only the land, houses and works of art but also chattels and jewels designated as heirlooms.

The novelist Anthony Trollope explained through Mr Dove, the lawyer in *The Eustace Diamonds* (1872), the high Victorian view that family treasures were preserved

not so much for the protection of property but for the more picturesque idea of maintaining chivalric associations. Heirlooms have become so, not that the future owners of them may be assured of so much wealth whatever the value of the things so settled may be − but that the son or grandson may enjoy the satisfaction of saying my father or grandfather or my ancestor sat in that chair or looked as he now looks in that picture or was graced by wearing on his breast that very ornament which you see lying beneath the glass.

It was in this spirit that the nobility tried to ensure that their family jewels were not dispersed. By his will of 1869 the twenty-fourth Earl of Crawford bequeathed all his diamonds and jewels to his successor in the earldom and in 1916 his grandson, the twenty-sixth Earl, made heirlooms of the diamonds which he had bought, 'with that specific intention and which

have been worn and adorned by my wife'. The Viscountess Curzon, who died in 1906, distinguished between her own personal jewels − which she left outright to her husband − and those which her father-in-law had given her when she married, which were to be returned to the eventual holder of the Kedleston title. Individual items of historic interest were protected in the same way, and in 1912 the tenth Baron St John of Bletso directed that the diamond and sapphire brooch presented to his grandfather Admiral Sir Richard Hussey in 1807 after the 'forcing of the Dardanelles' should devolve as a heirloom with his coronation robes.

On the rare occasions when jewels were bequeathed elsewhere then the holder of the title would try to buy them back. This happened when the famous Londonderry jewels were left by the fifth Marquess in 1884 to his third son Lord Herbert Vane-Tempest. The sixth Marquess persuaded his brother to sell and so the collection eventually passed to the seventh Marquess, with the exception of a diamond suite bequeathed to his sister Helen the Countess of Ilchester. Other fathers succumbed to the same temptation: the Lord Clifford of Chudleigh gave the family diamond stomacher to his favourite daughter the Hon. Lucy Clifford who married the nineteenth Baron Stourton in 1825 (Plate 241). The Clifford parure remains divided and the present Ladies Clifford· and Mowbray enjoy comparing their respective shares when they meet *en grande toilette* (Plates 242 and 243). It was customary of course for a mother's personal jewels to be shared by her daughters.

Plate 241. (*above*). Diamond foliate scroll and cluster stomacher with pendant fuschias removed from the Clifford parure and given to the Hon. Lucy Clifford, ancestress of Lord Mowbray, Segrave and Stourton, the present owner.

Plate 242 (*above*). Three oak leaf sprays remaining in the Clifford family: they can be worn as brooches or as hair ornaments.

Plate 243. The Clifford family diamond rivière, the stones graduated in size from the centre.

Dispersals

Dramatic changes accompanied the social and political upheavals which followed World War I. Smaller families mean there is often no direct heir, and titles have gone to distant cousins who have discovered that their inheritance does not include works of art and jewels which have been disposed of to daughters and friends. High taxation has been the reason for most dispersals, and jewellery, kept hidden away rather than worn because of the informality of modern social life which only rarely calls for its display, is particularly vulnerable. It is impossible to calculate how much has been sold through dealers as such information is confidential, but we do know that clients who tried to dispose of their possessions through Hennell's were not always successful because they asked unrealistically high prices. The Dowager Marchioness of Tweeddale demanded £3,000 for her eighteenth-century rose diamond and blue enamel buttons, commenting, 'absolutely unique, there is not such a complete set in or out of the country', and she also stipulated, 'They are not to be offered to Pierpont Morgan', then the most enthusiastic buyer of antique jewellery.

In 1927 the historic diamond necklace which Henry VIII's widow, Queen Katherine Parr, brought to her marriage with Sir Thomas Seymour was sold by Lady Sackville to Chaumet of Paris. It had been preserved untouched for hundreds of years until the eighteenth century when it was sold by the Seymour family and then reset. The wit and politician George Selwyn, who knew its history, acquired it as a wedding present for his ward Maria Fagniani when she married the future third Marquess of Hertford – a Seymour – in 1798. It descended through the fourth Marquess to his illegitimate son and heir, Sir Richard Wallace, whose widow left it to their secretary, the devoted Sir John Murray Scott. Fascinated by Lady Sackville, he bequeathed it in his turn to her – with many other Wallace art treasures – in the hope that it would become part of the ancestral collection at Knole, the great house of the Sackvilles in Kent.

Most jewellery has been sold at auction, the majority anonymously, but as the owner's name is sometimes published we do know the dates of some of the more important dispersals at Christie's. They are: the Temple diamonds (12 June 1929); the Earl of Crawford and Balcarres (31 July 1940); the Countess of Norbury – mainly pieces inherited from her great-

Plate 244. The Temple diamonds, with a pedigree going back to
1796, were sold in 1929.

grandmother, who married the fourth Duke of Portland in 1795 (2 March 1949 and 14 December 1953); the Marquess of Sligo (18 March 1953); the Duke of Newcastle (5 December 1958 and 4 October 1972); the Earl of Stanhope (4 May 1960), and the Countess Cadogan (5 July 1960) (see Plates 244-255). Many more ancestral jewels were sacrificed during World War I and World War II when sales were held to support the war effort and the Red Cross.

Plate 245. Diamond honeysuckle tiara formerly in the collection
of the Marquess of Sligo.

Plate 246. The Newcastle tiara with plume attached.

Plate 247. The Newcastle plume can be worn as a brooch.

Plate 248. Diamond tiara of roses in full bloom worn by Henrietta, wife of the fourth Duke of Portland.

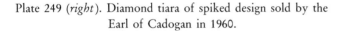

Plate 249 (*right*). Diamond tiara of spiked design sold by the Earl of Cadogan in 1960.

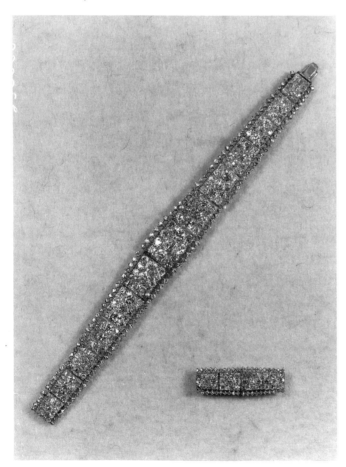

Plate 250. Diamond bracelet and brooch made from panels removed from an early-eighteenth century necklace, an heirloom of the Earl of Stanhope sold in 1960.

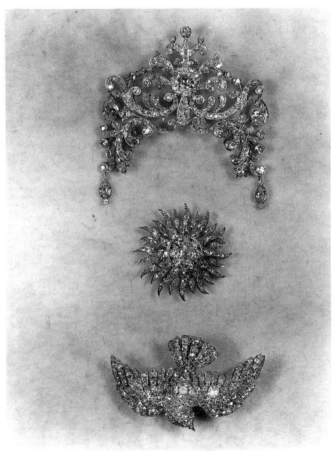

Plate 251. Newcastle heirlooms: an eighteenth-century pigeon brooch, a sunburst and a scrollwork stomacher brooch, sold in 1960.

Plate 252. Bouquet of flowers and ears of corn tied with diamond ribbons sold by the Earl of Cadogan.

Plate 253. Edwardian stomacher brooch worn by Adèle Countess of Essex, an American heiress.

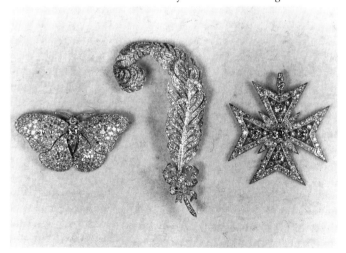

Plate 254. Diamond butterfly, plume and Maltese cross: English jewellery of the early nineteenth century sold by the Duke of Newcastle.

Plate 255. Diamond tiara worn by Lady Pole Carew.

Transformations

Once sold, either privately or at auction, jewels are almost always broken up and the stones remounted. This indeed has usually been their fate — as we have seen — when the stones have remained in the same family for generations. The young wife of today who does not think 'Granny's brooch' looks right with her St Laurent dress is only the latest in a long line of women who prefer up-to-date jewels, and sacrifice the old for this purpose. Only in exceptional cases were the settings preserved and paste substituted for precious stones: in 1912 Lady Hunter asked Hennell's to return the blue enamel settings 'as heirlooms' after removing the pearls from a pair of eighteenth-century earrings and a brooch, but most were indifferent.

Evidence of the various circumstances which led up to dispersals and remodelling can sometimes be found in family records. There is for instance in the Hackness family papers a lively account of the disappearance of the pearl necklace, diamond locket and other items which Queen Elizabeth gave her maid of honour, Elizabeth van Lore, daughter of Sir Peter van Lore, jeweller and dealer in precious stones. Elizabeth married the son of a prosperous Dutch banker, and their grandson, John van den Bempde, was so attached to these heirlooms that he separated from his wife Temperance after she pawned them to pay her gambling debts. His will of 1725-6, leaving his estate to their grandson, George, the future third Marquess of Annandale, demonstrates his concern, even though by that date the locket had been altered:

I desire that the pearl necklace, my diamond ring, my mother's picture done by Samuel Cooper in miniature sett in gold, my cousin Shelman's picture done by Sir Peter Lely may attend the family, especially the silver hilted sword of King Henry the 8th it being that with which he knighted the first of the Van den Bempdes that came over into England and brought £20,000 with them, whose son married a maid-of-honour to Queen Elizabeth who gave her the pearl necklace and diamond lockett of which the middle stone of my ring is one, the rest converted into the diamond buckle now in the custody of Sir Isaac Reboro.

Another early instance of the resetting of an important family gemstone can be seen in the 1689 will of Elizabeth Countess of Devonshire, who bequeathed her son William, the fourth Earl and future first Duke of Devonshire, 'my very best jewel being a very large breast jewel sett with diamonds in which jewel are (amongst many other diamonds) the large diamond which my late mother-in-law Christian gave me in a ring before my marriage'. Such transformations fascinated Alexander Pope who put into verse the previous history of Belinda's golden bodkin:

> The same his ancient personage to deck
> Her great-great grandsire wore about his neck
> In three seal rings, which, after melted down
> Formed one huge buckle for his widow's gown.

Statesmen and officers removed the diamonds from presentation swords, snuff boxes and miniatures to set in jewels for their wives. If they did not, then later generations were often tempted to do so. Thus the diamonds in the hilt of the sword presented by George III to Admiral Lord Howe in July 1794 to commemorate the victory of the 'Glorious First of June' (Plate 256) were removed in this century to make a pair of bracelets (Plate 257). The fine diamonds

Plate 256. Portrait of Admiral Viscount Howe standing beside his ceremonial sword, painted by J. Harrison.

in the sword given by Ferdinand IV, King of Naples and Sicily, to Admiral Viscount Nelson after his victory at the Battle of the Nile were remounted by his niece Lady Bridport into a necklace. Sold at Christie's in July 1895, they were acquired by the Earl of Mexborough and illustrated in the 11 April 1952 issue of *Country Life*.

Plate 257. Viscountess Howe photographed by Paul Tanqueray wearing bracelets set with stones removed from hilt of the Howe cermonial sword.

Documents at the estate office of Newtonwards near Mountstewart in Ulster tell the story of the remounting of the Londonderry diamonds in the 1850s, which resulted in the creation of the famous parure worn by the reigning Marchioness ever since (Plate 259). It was kept apart from the rest of the collection in a stout rosewood box inlaid with brass, inscribed on the inside of the lid THE DOWN DIAMONDS. Some had been brought into the family by Mary Cowan, who married Sir Alexander Stewart

in 1737 and was heiress to her nabob half-brother Robert, for many years Governor of Bombay. The numerous Brazilian gems were gifts from allied monarchs to the eminent statesman, Viscount Castlereagh – later second Marquess of Londonderry – at the time of the Congress of Vienna in 1814. According to Mrs Arbuthnot's *Journal*, he cut a splendid figure at the coronation of King George IV in 1821, with diamonds flashing out from the hilt of his sword, from his hat band, his George and Garter star: 'the people echoed his name from one to the other the whole length of the platform and received him with repeated cheers. It was unanimously voted that he was the handsomest man in the procession'. No less than 1,225 brilliant-cut diamonds were mounted into the wide belt which encircles the waist

Plate 258. Portrait of Emily, wife of the second Marquess of Londonderry, wearing diamond belt, shoulder clasps and bandeau, painted by Sir Thomas Lawrence.

of the black velvet dress his wife Emily wears in a portrait by Sir Thomas Lawrence (Plate 258). Viscount Castlereagh was devoted to her and in a letter dated 17 August 1818 he told her that, although the diamonds were eventually to go as heirlooms with the marquessate, during her lifetime she had the right to dispose of them as she wished:

My dearest Emily,

As political events in other countries have shaken Private Property (an event which in this happy country can hardly be apprehended) but as in such a case I wish your ease and comfort to be provided for in preference to all other considerations, I have therefore bequeathed to your absolute disposal the Diamonds and beg you will not hesitate in such case to apply them to your own use. If the occasion should not occur it is my wish that they should be considered as Memorials in the Family of the Public Transactions most of which you have shared with me as Witness.

He died first, and on her death in 1829, as they had no children, the diamonds passed to his brother Charles, the third Marquess. In 1854 they were remounted in one spectacular parure by Robert Garrard,

the crown jeweller, for the Marchioness, Frances Anne. First, as they were heirlooms, permission to alter the settings had to be obtained from Frederick, the future fourth Marquess and, when this was given, Garrards were asked to submit designs and estimates. Their estimate, dated 21 July 1854, sets out the proposed alterations and cost:

Resetting brilliants from waistband as tiara to divide as comb and brooches (£512)

Resetting brilliants as pair of hair pins (£20)

Resetting brilliants from star badge and sword as stomacher brooch to divide into three brooches (£175)

Resetting brilliants from bracelet, clasp and necklace as two bracelets (£150)

Resetting brilliants from necklace and sword hilt as corsage to act also as necklace (£175)

This came to a total of £1,032. The diamonds were listed by number and weight and valued at £16,863.8s. and the account was settled in December 1855. An additional charge of £82.13s. was made for replacing the diamonds taken from the Castlereagh Garter insignia with false stones, 'for the sake of preserving

the form and pattern of the original work', which had made such an impression at the coronation in 1821. The blue velvet Garter with diamond motto was not touched. The parure made from the Down diamonds illustrates British jewellery of the Great Exhibition period at its best, for the quality is excellent and the magnificent stones are designed to tremble with each movement. The celebrated Edwardian hostess Marchioness Theresa and her daughter-in-law, Marchioness Edith, wore it to the manner born – as if there was nothing unusual in the possession of such treasures (Plate 259).

Gifts of diamonds from Indian princes to King George III and Queen Charlotte were sold by their executors to the court jewellers, Rundell, Bridge and Rundell. A round brilliant – which could be the Hastings diamond given to the King by the Nizam Ali Cawn through Warren Hastings as intermediary and lent by Rundell and Bridge to George IV for his coronation crown – the two almond-shaped drops presented to Queen Charlotte by the Nawab of Arcot set in a bracelet, and a pair of

Plate 259 (left). Theresa, wife of the sixth Marquess of Londonderry, wearing the diamond parure made by Robert Garrard in 1854 from stones removed from Marchioness Emily's jewels and the second Marquess's insignia.

Plate 260. The Londonderry Latin cross and necklace worn by Marchioness Theresa in plate 259.

Plate 261. Tiara made by Lacloche set with the two pear-shaped Arcot diamonds and
a large round brilliant bought by the Marquess of Westminster in 1837.

earrings were bought by the Marquess of Westminster in 1837. He wore the three stones in his Garter star and sword hilt during the state visit of Louis-Philippe in 1844. Thereafter the Arcot and Hastings diamonds underwent further transformations until the second Duke of Westminster had them set in a tiara by the Paris firm of Lacloche (Plate 261). The round brilliant in the centre was detachable and could be worn as a brooch and the two Arcots as earrings. Cecil Beaton photographed Duchess Loelia – the Duke's third wife – with this tiara in 1931 (Plate 262), and Duchess Anne – his fourth wife – wore it to the coronation of 1953. When the second Duke died the tiara was sold, at Sotheby's on 25 June 1959. It was bought by the New York jeweller, Harry Winston, who removed the three principal stones and sold them as solitaire rings. The tiara, which was not broken up, was recently sold, again by Sotheby's, in New York on 17 October 1988.

Smaller and less important items were transformed too. In 1858 the Countess of Carlisle left her eldest daughter, Lady Dover, 'the brooch of different coloured stones given me by George IV when Prince

of Wales' at her christening of 1804, 'which had some small ornaments hanging from it which I had made into earrings and which may also be given to her if they can be found'. The amethyst and diamond cluster brooch pinned to the feathers in Lady Peel's black velvet hat and which she wears in her portrait by Sir Thomas Lawrence (Plate 133), was inherited by her daughter, the Hon. Mrs Francis Stonor, and when it descended to Jeanne, the late Dowager Lady Camoys, she had it mounted as a ring. At Burghley House a Victorian emerald and diamond heart locket has also been made into a ring, and both look more impressive on the finger than would be the case if they were pinned to a dress, or hung round the neck.

Quantities of diamonds were removed from eighteenth-century jewels and set in the Devonshire parure in order to lighten the massive effect of so many cameos as the jeweller, C.F. Hancock, explained to Sir Joseph Paxton, agent of the sixth Duke of Devonshire. In their turn the larger stones were used in jewels ordered by the former Duchess of Manchester, Louise, who married the eighth Duke in 1892. Her most important commission was a diadem,

Plate 262. Loelia Duchess of Westminister, wearing the Lacloche tiara in a photograph by Cecil Beaton taken in 1931. The tiara was sold in 1959.

Plate 263. Duchess Evelyn, wife of the ninth Duke of Devonshire, Mistress of
the Robes to Queen Mary. She wears the honeysuckle diadem set with
diamonds from old family pieces including the Devonshire parure,
made for her predecessor, Duchess Louise.

Plate 264. Lady Sackville wearing the Cartier tasselled tiara set
with diamonds removed from an eighteenth-century Sackville family necklace.

supplied by A.E. Skinner of Orchard Street, consisting of 'twelve honeysuckle ornaments with fourteen between pieces resting on a two-row bandeau with collets between'. It was set with 1,907 diamonds, '1,041 belonging to his Grace broken from old ornaments' and, as had been the case with the Londonderry diamonds, all were listed by number and weight. A letter from the Duchess Louise, at Chatsworth, mentions that five large rubies which she had set into brooches and in the clasp of one of her pearl necklaces (see chapter 6, page 144) came from the St George's cross in the Garter star given by George IV to the fifth Duke in 1821. It was one of four ordered from Rundell, Bridge and Rundell: the others were for the King himself, the Marquess of Hertford and the Duke of Wellington. The Duchess also wrote,

the pearl necklace was found in a box at the bank, and the best pearls in my necklace were added to it, and the brilliant clasp was a ring we found in Bedford Square in an old bureau belonging to Lord Charles and Lady Anne Cavendish. [Lord Charles was the son of the second Duke who married Lady Anne Grey, daughter of the Duke of Kent in 1727.] A pair of pearl drop earrings with brilliant

tops were the old Duchess of Devonshire's [wife of the third Duke] and left to Lord Frederick [Lord Frederick Cavendish, who died 1803] by whom they came to Lord George. [Lord George Cavendish first Earl of Burlington, grandfather of the eighth Duke].

Edwardian ladies who continued to wear old-fashioned ornaments were criticised by the novelist Elinor Glyn in 1908, impressed by the elegance of Americans who 'crossed the Atlantic twice a year to have their dresses fitted, and whose jewels were perfect, not a bit like the English sticking to their hideous early Victorian settings'. But many did exchange their ancestral pieces for delicate garland-style jewels in platinum mounts. Lady Sackville removed the stones from the famous 'collier de la Reine' acquired in 1790 by the third Duke of Dorset for his bride Arabella and which had descended with the Knole estate to her husband. Cartier reset the stones in a tiara of festoon and tassel design for her (Plate 264). The sixth Marquess of Londonderry gave the Antrim rubies as a wedding present to his daughter-in-law, later Marchioness Edith, in 1899. She had them reset in a necklace/bandeau, a pair of earrings, ribbon style stomacher, ring and wrist watch which she first wore in 1906 to the wedding of Alphonso XIII and Princess Ena in Madrid. This is still in the family. By the time of the first court of the reign of King George V in 1911, the Hon. Katherine Villiers, a maid of honour, observed that it was only the elderly dowagers who still wore antique jewellery.

The process never ended. In 1936 *Vogue* reported that 'the Duchess of Buccleuch, Lady Brownlow, and several other important English women are starting a new fashion by having their heirloom solitaire diamond necklaces made choker length. Old-fashioned diamond flower pins and stars are being revived as clips and refitted with modern fastenings.'

Loss and Theft

As least as much damage has been done by fire as by the whims of humans. In 1835 when the west wing of Hatfield House was burnt down the octogenarian widow of the first Marquess of Salisbury was killed and all her jewels lost. During World War II countless family treasures were destroyed when bank vaults were bombed and all who kept their jewels with Spink and Co. lost them when that firm was hit during the Blitz.

Even the most careful people lose jewellery, whether earrings (Plate 265), small rings or large bracelets. Among the notes which Marchioness Edith made for the album of the Londonderry jewels at Mount Stewart was a hair-raising account of the disappearance of one of the Antrim emeralds:

The jewels belonging to the Antrim family, which became the property of Frances Anne, included a very beautiful parure of diamonds and emeralds of magnificent colour and size. They formed a tiara or could be worn across a dress as they are really too large for a necklace. Theresa, Lady Londonderry, my mother-in-law, lost the most important brooch which belonged to this set. It was a very large square emerald with large diamond leaves like those of an acanthus plant.

She wore it one evening when going to a reception at Sunderland House and drove there in her brougham. It was only just around the corner from Londonderry House, at the junction of Curzon and Hertford Street. She was

Plate 265. Portrait of Mrs George Augustus Frederick Cavendish Bentinck by G.F. Watts. She lost one of the eighteenth-century carnival mask earrings she is wearing, and had the other mounted in the lid of a box.

not feeling very well at the time and went straight up the stairs and shook hands with the Duchess of Marlborough, leaving a very short while afterwards. On the way downstairs she put up her hand and found the brooch missing. Although a great search was made for it, it was never seen again. From the size of the ornament it could not have fallen down into a chink and the surmise is that it must have been picked up by one of the guests!

If true, this was not a new development, for theft has always been the greatest hazard. In the eighteenth century thieves were so active at court that no one who lost a stone from its setting there ever expected to see it again. Lord Mexborough's Garter badge was cut from his ribbon and Sir George Warren's diamond Bath star disappeared at King George III's birthday Drawing Room.

Town and country houses were raided regularly. There was a great sensation in 1835 when the jewel chest of the Duchess of Gordon was taken from the dressing room of her Belgrave Square house while the Duke was out at dinner. Queen Adelaide sent some of her own jewels in a gesture of sympathy and

Plate 226. The Northumberland strawberry leaf tiara set with diamonds from the ceremonial sword
given to the third Duke by King George IV. It was stolen in 1963.

the philosophical Duchess declared that as a result of the disaster she was at last free from the worry of valuable possessions. Burglars at Charlecote in Warwickshire in 1850 made off with a collection of watches and chatelaines: among them was the fine repeater which had descended from the first Sir Thomas Lucy and the irreplaceable watch with his miniature on the dial which Charles II had given Jane Lane who had helped him escape after the Battle of Worcester.

In May 1875 Lord Beaconsfield told Lady Bradford, 'all Lady Churchill's jewels were robbed from an Albemarle Street hotel where she has put up for many years and a little while ago Lady Waterpark lost all her jewels. "Two of my ladies", the Queen indignantly exclaims, "the police must be very inefficient. It is a disgrace to the country".' The spate of robberies continued nonetheless. Diamonds and sapphires were stolen from Lord Eldon's country home in 1880, and honeymoon couples were particularly vulnerable, as lists of wedding presents were published in the newspapers. While staying at Halsted

Place in the country after their wedding in 1877, the Earl and Countess of Aberdeen were burgled and she recalled years later,

heedless of warnings I had brought with me most of my wedding presents and all the treasured ornaments which had been lavished on me during my childhood by my parents and a large circle of relations and friends. They took my precious pearl and diamond necklace, the big diamond and sapphire locket from my husband, and a lovely old chatelaine in the form of an enamelled egg with miniature globe inside ornamented with a coronet and containing a blood red heart — his gift on the day of the wedding.

This was a warning to all and rigorous precautions were taken to safeguard the jewels of the Countesses of Dalhousie and Rosebery, and the Duchess of Norfolk, when they married shortly after. It was during this period that advertisements for Chubb's safes began to appear regularly in the papers. No system in infallible: some years ago the strong room at Carrington's in Regent Street was emptied just after a new alarm had been installed.

Plate 267. Enamelled gold George studded with rose-cut diamonds, given by Queen Anne to the first Duke of Marlborough, and returned to King George IV who gave it to the Duke of Wellington. Stolen in 1965.

Plate 268. Diamond badge of the Order of the Golden Fleece with ruby-tipped flames. The Condesa de Chinchon, granddaughter of Philip V, gave it to the Duke of Wellington. Stolen in 1965.

Sometimes the unfortunate victim was robbed away from home. Coming back from the theatre in 1755 a Mrs Hodges of Hanover Square was relieved of £1,000 worth of jewels by a particularly audacious thief who, pistol in hand, had been waiting for her, hidden beneath the seat of her coach. And in 1777 Mrs Lybbe Powys remarked that the area around Henley was teeming with highwaymen intent on seizing diamonds. It was the same abroad and in 1814 Nancy Parsons, wife of the second Viscount Maynard, and her French lover were murdered in the forest of Fontainebleau by thieves who took the family jewels from them. The stones came onto the Paris market, and according to some experts, the 'well-known

Maynard rivière' was among the jewels of the Empress Eugénie sold by the Third Republic in 1887.

The twentieth-century thief is just as adept as the eighteenth-century highwayman. In 1920, while at St Pancras station, the Countess of Verulam was robbed of the lovely suite of diamonds which the first Earl had given his bride Lady Charlotte Jenkinson on their marriage in 1807. And, in a rather sinister development, during the 1920s, thieves resorted to administering drugs to their wealthy victims.

In April 1959 the Duchess of Rutland travelled from London in a crowded railway compartment: on arrival at Belvoir Castle her maid noticed that the jewel case was missing from the luggage. It was never found and with it went jewels which had escaped a previous Rutland burglary in London eleven years before. Another great loss was the theft of the Northumberland jewels from the Duchess Helen, Mistress of the Robes to Queen Elizabeth the Queen Mother, as she was bringing them home from Robert Garrard, the crown jeweller: she was to wear them for the state banquet to be given by the King and Queen of Greece at Claridges that evening, 11 July 1963 (Plate 266). As she arrived at her Eaton Square home six men held up the car and took the two boxes from the seat beside her. Similarly irreplaceable were the Sutherland jewels, stolen from their hiding place while the fifth Duke and Duchess Claire were at dinner.

Even the national collections are not secure and public ownership is no deterrent. The insignia of the Duke of Wellington – the George which King George IV gave him and which had been the Duke of Marlborough's (Plate 267), and the diamond and ruby Golden Fleece from the Condesa de Chinchon (Plate 268), granddaughter of Philip V of Spain – were stolen from Apsley House on 9 December 1965.

Such a catalogue of disasters makes one appreciate the true value of the jewels described in this book. The odds against survival are heavy indeed and if it were not for those generations who have held fast to them, these most precious and personal links with the great names of our past would have been lost. Their persistence deserves our gratitude.

Plate 269. The Dudley lion made by Cartier in 1968-9. The eyes are set with rubies and the coat paved with yellow diamonds. This lively English heraldic brooch was stolen from Grace Countess of Dudley in 1973.

GLOSSARY

Aigrette Jewel for hat or hair, usually imitating feathers and flowers (see Plate 67).

Arabesque Fanciful stylised line ornament of scrolling and interlaced foliage derived from Islamic art; usually symmetrical (see Plate 5).

Bezel The focal point of a finger ring, seen on the top of the finger (see Plate 87).

Brilliant Diamond that is brilliant-cut (*see below*).

Brilliant-cut A diamond cut with fifty-six facets around the table and culet so as to produce the maximum brilliance from the stone.

Bright-cut Type of decoration typical of Neo-classical gold and silverwork, achieved by cutting sharply into the metal at an angle and then giving it a high polish to contrast with the surround.

Cabochon The domed surface of a stone which has not been faceted (see Plate 38).

Cameo A hardstone engraved so that the image stands out in relief (see Plate 7).

Carbuncle Cabochon almandine garnet.

Chrysoprase Apple-green coloured hardstone (see Plate 131).

Collet Metal recess into which stone is set.

Crocketed Crested, like the steep sloping pinnacles of mediaeval architecture (see Plate 132).

Demi-parure Suite of two pieces, usually earrings and brooch, matching in material and design (see Plate 154).

Dog-collar Choker worn high on the throat composed of rows of pearls kept in place by diamond bars or centre plaque; introduced into English jewellery by Queen Alexandra when Princess of Wales (see Plate 197).

Esclavage Section of chain or stones linked to others in a necklace like the fetters of a slave.

Etui Case containing useful objects − scissors, tweezers, etc., usually worn hanging on a chatelaine.

Festoon Hanging like a garland of fruit or flowers (see Plate 124).

Gimmel Twin ring composed of two hoops joined at the base which open on a pivot, but when closed looks like one.

Girandole Earring with three pendent drops branching out from a top section (see Plate 66).

Intaglio Hardstone engraved with the image below the surface so that an impression can be taken from it for sealing.

Moss agate Hardstone with inclusions simulating the natural forms of plants, shrubs and trees (see Plate 87).

Negligée Necklace without clasps but which terminates in tassels falling over the shoulders (see Plate 126).

Parure Complete suite of necklace, earrings, brooches, head ornaments, etc., matching in design and material (see Plate 149).

Rivière River of stones linked together in a string for necklace (see Plate 243).

Rose-cut Diamond with faceting over the surface so that stone looks like a rosebud. Used in the seventeenth and early-eighteenth centuries (see Plate 29) then superseded by the brilliant-cut (*see above*).

Sardonyx Hardstone of three layers of contrasting colours used for cameos (see Plate 6).

Sautoir Long chain of beads, precious stones or pearls several feet long.

Scrollwork Curvilinear designs (see Plate 37).

Sévigné Jewelled bowknot pinned to the centre of neckline, named in the nineteenth century after the famous seventeenth-century letter writer Madame de Sévigné who wears one in a portrait (see Plate 167).

Slide Medallion, sometimes containing a miniature or lock of hair, with raised loops at the back through which a ribbon can be threaded for wear at neck or wrist (see Plates 57 and 58).

Stomacher Large brooch filling the space between low neckline and waist (see Plate 253).

Table-cut A stone which has been sliced across the top, leaving the surface flat (see Plate 40).

Top and drop Earrings designed in two parts, the pendent drop swinging from a top section which covers the lobe (see Plate 122).

SELECT BIBLIOGRAPHY

Exhibition Catalogues

1. Loan Exhibition of Ancient and Modern Jewellery, Victoria and Albert Museum, 1872.

2. Exhibition of the Royal House of Stuart, New Gallery, London, 1889.

3. Exhibition of the Royal House of Tudor, New Gallery, London, 1890.

4. Exhibition of the Four Georges, 25 Park Lane, 1931.

5. Exhibition of the Ageless Diamond, Christie's, 1959.

6. Exhibition of Gemstones and Jewellery, City of Birmingham Museum and Art Gallery, 1960.

7. Dix Siècles de Joaillerie Française, Musée du Louvre, Paris, 1962.

8. Further Wellington Gems and Historic Rings, S.J. Phillips, Bond Street, London, 1978.

9. Princely Magnificence, Court Jewels of the Renaissance, Victoria and Albert Museum, 1980.

10. The Grosvenor Treasures, Sotheby's, Chester, 1984.

11. Treasures from British Houses, National Gallery of Art, Washington, 1984.

12. The Countess's Gems, Burghley House, 1985.

Published Works

E. Bancroft, *Letters from England 1846–1849* (1904).

A. Calder-Marshall, *The Two Duchesses* (1978).

Catalogue of the Ornamental Furniture, Works of Art and Porcelain at Welbeck Abbey (Privately Printed, 1897).

L. Cohen, *Lady de Rothschild and Her Daughters 1821–1931* (1935).

E. Collier (ed.), *Later Extracts from the Journal of Mary Lady Monkswell 1895–1909* (1946).

The Journal of Lady Mary Coke (Kingsmead Reprints, Bath, 1970).

E. De Clermont-Tonnère, *Mémoires Au Temps des Equipages* (1928).

Oliver, Viscount Esher (ed.), *Diaries of Viscount Esher, Vol. IV* (1938).

B. Fitzgerald (ed.), *Correspondence of Emily Duchess of Leinster 1731–1814*, I (1949) II (1953), III (1957).

George Fox, 'Account of the Firm of Rundell, Bridge and Rundell', Unpublished Ms., completed 1846, in Baker Library, Harvard, USA.

Lady Llanover (ed.), *The Autobiography and Correspondence of Mrs. Delany* (1861).

Hans Nadelhoffer, *Cartier* (1984).

Richard Rush, *A Residence at the Court of London 1819–1825* (1873).

D. Scarisbrick, 'The Devonshire Parure', *Archaeologia*, Vol. 108 (1986), pp. 239–54.

C. Eastlake Smith, *Journals and Correspondence of Lady Eastlake* (1895).

H. Tait, *The Waddesdon Bequest* (1986).

INDEX